Evil Women

DEADLIER THAN THE MALE

John Marlowe

This edition published in 2012 by Arcturus Publishing Limited
26/27 Bickels Yard, 151–153 Bermondsey Street,
London SE1 3HA

This edition published in Australia by Hinkler Books Pty Ltd,
45-55 Fairchild Street, Heatherton, Victoria 3202 Australia

AD002439EN

Printed in the UK

Contents

CONTENTS

Introduction

This book is about some of the evil acts that have been committed by wives, girlfriends and common-law wives. It contains stories of deceit, betrayal and, ultimately, murder. The victims of these women are more often than not family members: mothers, fathers, sisters, brothers and, in almost every case, husbands.

All of the murderers presented here were caught and each one of them received justice of a sort. Most of these criminals initially denied any involvement in the crimes that they had committed, despite being faced by overwhelming evidence to the contrary. However, many of them eventually came up with interesting explanations, even excuses, for their actions.

It is said that no one is innocent. We are reminded of this many times over by the various defences mounted on behalf of the accused. Victims are often made to share the blame for their demise, as was the case in the murder of Pastor Matthew Winkler. After admitting that she was guilty of his murder, the dead man's wife expressed her wish that the reputation of the pastor, 'a mighty fine person', should not be tarnished. Yet, during the subsequent trial she did just that.

Contradicting her statement to the police, Mary Carol Winkler portrayed her dead husband as a physically abusive pervert. Winkler's testimony was strikingly similar to the statements of other women who have been accused of killing their spouses. Many of their victims were depicted as dark individuals with heavily guarded secret lives. Husbands with no history of violence suddenly became physically abusive brutes, who often made their wives engage in sexual practices that they found distasteful.

This treatment is not limited to spouses, nor is it exclusively meted out to the dead.

When Marie Hilley was accused of murdering her husband, mother and mother-in-law with arsenic the evidence against her was overwhelming. Yet she did not hesitate to blacken her daughter's character. Hilley's lawyers attempted to explain the high levels of arsenic in her daughter's system by portraying the young woman as an unstable, drug-addicted, suicidal lesbian, who was more than capable of poisoning herself. Marie's use of poison is reminiscent of a time when women had a reputation for being 'quiet killers'. Poisoning was once the preferred method of female murderers. No more. The arsenic-laced plum cakes and coffee that were served by Nannie Doss between the 1920s and 1954 have been replaced by handguns, shotguns and knives.

One thing that has not changed in recent decades is motive. The vast majority of murders committed by women are carried out for profit. This is particularly true of female serial killers. On the other hand, men are often sexually motivated when they commit murder. The methods adopted by male and female serial killers are also significantly different. While men prey on strangers, women tend to murder those who depend upon them in some capacity, including immediate family members.

Many people find it difficult to believe that women are capable of serial murder so female killers have often been able to avoid apprehension for extended periods. Thus,

Dorothea Puente was permitted to leave her property and disappear, even as bodies were being excavated in her back garden. It is unlikely that a man would have received the same treatment. Likewise, it seems inconceivable that Marie Hilley could have avoided suspicion had she not been a woman.

The concept of the evil wife seems so much more shocking than that of the evil husband, perhaps because women are so closely associated with nurture and support in western society. In the case of most women society's trust is not misplaced, but one must be ready to accept that there are always exceptions.

John Marlowe
Montreal, Quebec

JANE ANDREWS
from Buckingham Palace
to life imprisonment

Although she was brought up in modest circumstances – she was the daughter of a carpenter and his social worker wife – Jane Andrews would enjoy a lavish lifestyle that included extensive travel. Because she was attractive and intelligent, she was able to secure a position with a member of the royal family when she was very young. However, the personality that had gained her entry to Buckingham Palace would show itself to have a dark and dangerous side. What had begun as a fairy tale ended in a scene worthy of a horror film.

Jane was born in Cleethorpes, in North East Lincolnshire, in 1967. She was the youngest of three children. Both of her parents worked, which was not so common in those days. It was necessary, though, because full-time employment was a rarity for Jane's father. As time progressed, and the family's debts grew, Jane's parents were forced to sell their home. When she was eight years old her family moved to Grimsby, where they settled into a cramped terraced house with an outside lavatory. The move to cheaper accommodation did little to alleviate the family's financial pressures. Jane recalled one instance in which she and her siblings were told to look around the house for loose change so that their mother might buy a loaf of bread. This lack of money led to frequent arguments, so Jane found it increasingly difficult to concentrate on her school homework. Perhaps unsurprisingly, she did not always fit the description of a good student, even though she achieved high grades.

TROUBLED TEEN

At the age of 15, she was caught playing truant. After a social services worker had informed her mother, Jane swallowed a cocktail of the pills she had found in the family medicine cabinet. Even though her mother quickly realized what Jane had done, she did not call an ambulance. Jane would remain in her bedroom, slipping in and out of consciousness until she finally recovered. Her parents were adamant that the suicide attempt would not be made public. The incident had no effect on Jane's truancy. In a relatively short time, she had destroyed what might have been a successful academic career. She ended up at the Grimsby College of Art, where she studied fashion design.

Jane had been sexually active with a number of partners since the age of 15. Perhaps it was small wonder, then, that she became pregnant while she was attending the Grimsby college. However, the abortion that followed caused her a great deal of mental trauma.

After graduating from college the best she could manage was a job as a sales assistant at Marks & Spencer in Grimsby. It did not appear to be the sort of work that offered much of a future, so she kept on looking for the right opening. In 1988 she answered an anonymous advertisement in *The Lady* magazine: it was for a personal dresser. Six months passed before Jane received a response. As it turned out, the advertisement had been taken out on behalf of the Duchess of York. Jane was summoned for an interview, which she passed with flying colours. She began her employment as personal dresser to the duchess in July 1988, one month before the birth of Princess Beatrice.

So a poor girl who had arrived at Buckingham Palace with nothing more than £10 and a suitcase soon found herself in daily contact with members of the royal family. After having lived the first 21 years of her life in conditions of near-poverty, Jane was enjoying fine food and luxurious accommodation. For the first time in her life money was a pleasure, not a problem. As personal dresser to the duchess she was able to buy a car and she always had plenty of cash to spend on clothing of her own. 'Lady Jane', as she was called by the duchess, had been in royal employment for just under a year when she met an IBM executive named Christopher Dunn-Butler. Born in 1946, he was more than two decades her senior, yet this age difference appeared to be no obstacle. A whirlwind romance followed. Three months after the two had met, Jane had an engagement ring on her finger. The couple married in August of 1990, but things gradually soured.

INFIDELITY

Jane had already had several affairs when she met Dimitri Horne, a Greek shipping magnate, at a charity function. Eventually, she left her husband and took up residence in a flat that the duchess had rented on her behalf. Citing infidelity, Christopher sued for divorce. When the marriage between the duchess and Prince Andrew began to dissolve, Jane was kept on and was given added responsibilities. The two women continued to be close friends, travelling the globe together and sharing confidences. As news of the royal break-up consumed the tabloids, Jane's less public relationship with Dimitri was also coming to an end. After the shipping magnate had told her that it was over, Jane visited his flat when he was not at home. She smashed his possessions, struck out all references to herself in his journal and wrote herself a cheque on his brother's account.

Jane's actions towards her ex-boyfriend were not totally out of character. She had made death threats against one former lover and had vandalized his car. She had telephoned another past partner to tell him that she was in an abortion clinic and would proceed with the operation if he did not come back to her. In fact, she was not even pregnant. Jane took an overdose of pills after that episode, but she survived without the need of medical intervention. Life might have seemed unbearable, but it would only get worse.

In November 1997, when she was in her tenth year as the duchess's dresser, Jane was suddenly dismissed. The termination came as a great shock to her. It was all the more difficult to accept when the duchess allowed someone else to give her the bad news. While the reason given for the abrupt dismissal was cost-cutting, Jane's finances fell under scrutiny. Her salary was a modest £18,000 a year and yet she had managed to purchase an expensive London flat and amass some £50,000 in savings. The *Independent* quoted a palace official as saying, 'It was never proved legally, but we are convinced she stole a huge amount of money'.

Another factor had perhaps contributed to Jane's dismissal. She had told other members of the royal household that Count Gaddo della Gheradecsu, an Italian aristocrat with whom the duchess was friendly, had been paying her some attention. Jane was deeply depressed at this point so it was some time before she managed to find another job. In the end, she was hired by the upmarket London jewellery firm Annabel Jones, where she worked in the silver department.

Then in August 1998 she met a well-connected businessman named Tom Cressman.

The couple had been introduced by a mutual friend, after which the charismatic businessman insisted on driving Jane home. After learning that his passenger was flying off to Greece the next day, he made certain that she was met with red roses on her return.

Despite such a promising beginning, though, it seemed that Jane and Tom were not all that compatible. The 39-year-old businessman relished his bachelor lifestyle, while his new girlfriend seemed keen on marriage. There were other factors, too. According to Jane, Tom enjoyed anal sex, bondage and role-playing, all of which she considered disgusting. The friction between them was such, according to Jane, that each of them threatened to expose the other's secrets. Jane was going to tell her boyfriend's business associates about his sexual predilections, while Tom was ready to go to the tabloids with a series of juicy stories about Jane's time with the duchess.

A few months into the relationship, Jane broke her wrist while dancing with Tom. Although she thought he had injured her deliberately, Jane accepted his offer to stay at his west London flat while the injury healed. But Jane had no intention of leaving once she had moved in. The unhealthy relationship came to an end in September 2000.

According to Jane's account, Tom had finally accepted the idea of marriage. However, the evidence suggests otherwise. Early in the month, Jane and Tom attended a boat show in Italy, followed by a visit to the Cressman family villa on the French Riviera. It was at some point during the trip that Tom bluntly informed Jane that he would never marry her.

THE FINAL ASSAULT

On the final day, Jane drove to the Aéroport Nice Côte d'Azur with Tom's mother and his nephew. Her mobile telephone conversations could be clearly overheard. She was telling her friends that the relationship was through.

And yet she returned home with Tom. Jane later claimed that Tom had undergone a change of heart on the flight back to England and that he had even gone so far as to agree to seek counselling for his sexual interests. However, by the next morning, 16 September, Tom had reconsidered his position. According to Jane's testimony, Tom tied her up and anally raped her before ordering her out of his flat. A physical fight ensued, during which Tom was driven to call a police telephone operator for help.

> Tom: 'I would like someone to stop us hurting each other. If you don't have somebody here soon somebody is —'
> Operator: 'Right, Mr Cressman?'
> Tom: 'Yes.'
> Operator: 'All right, what are you wanting your partner to do? What are you arguing about?'

Tom: 'Our relationship.'

Operator: 'Do you not think it would be better you discuss it when you both calm down?'

Tom: 'I would love to discuss it calmed down. She will not.'

Operator: 'Do you want her to leave?'

Tom: 'Yes.'

Operator: 'Right, what you should do, sir, arrange for her to find suitable accommodation.'

Tom: 'I would love to do that.'

Operator: 'That's not something the police can provide for you.'

Tom: 'No.'

Operator: 'That's something you will have to discuss calmly. I will get the police to come and see both of you – all they will do is advise you regarding your behaviour. There's nothing specific we can do – we are not a marriage guidance service, we deal with crime.'

But no help arrived. The calls that were recorded on Jane's mobile phone indicate that she had left the flat by noon. Although the recipient of most of the calls was Tom, Jane was also communicating with his parents. While she had been away from the house, Jane had emailed them copies of the sexually-charged correspondence that Tom had exchanged with Deborah DiMicelli, an American woman he had met at a conference in Las Vegas some months earlier.

And yet, despite it all, Jane returned to Tom. Why?

According to Jane, the violence of the morning had seemed unreal. In her account, the last evening they spent together featured another attempt at anal sex, after which Tom had fallen asleep. She was not certain whether or not she too was sleeping when Tom suddenly begun beating her. He was yelling, 'I'm going to f***ing kill you'. Jane said that she managed to grab a cricket bat and a kitchen knife – both of which she had earlier carried upstairs – and then she lashed back. The cricket bat struck Tom on the head, after which he pulled at Jane's hair, and then – somehow – fell on to the eight-inch knife. With life draining from his body, Tom failed in his struggle to remove the knife from his chest.

Jane's recollection of Tom's death was extremely sketchy,

as were the moments that followed. She did not remember showering, though the evidence clearly indicated that she had. How long she remained in the house is unknown but before leaving she scrawled a note: 'Tom hurt me too much. He was so cruel to me'. Tom's body was discovered two days later, when an employee visited his house. In the meantime, Jane had been texting her friends. Among those she contacted was the Duchess of York, who asked her to turn herself in. Then four days after the murder she was found curled up in the back seat of her white Volkswagen Polo, suffering from yet another overdose.

How much, if anything, the jury believed of Jane's story of abuse at the hands of the man she so wanted to marry is, perhaps, reflected in its verdict. The judge had instructed the jury that they could acquit Jane of the charges if they decided that Tom's death was an accident or that she had acted in self-defence. Alternatively, a verdict of manslaughter could be considered if they felt that Jane had been provoked or had suffered from diminished responsibility. In the end, however, the jury determined that Jane was guilty of murder.

On 16 May 2001, the former dresser to the duchess of York was sentenced to life imprisonment.

TRACIE ANDREWS
The 'road rage'
killer

The earliest reports painted a picture that was as disturbing as it was gruesome. On the evening of 1 December 1996, Lee Harvey, a young English father, had been butchered beside his white Ford Escort. He had been stabbed 15 times and his throat had been slashed. The dead man was seen as a victim of road rage. 'He died in the arms of his fiancée,' reported *The Times*. His fiancée, Tracie Andrews, appeared at a news conference two days afterwards. The 27-year-old woman was a former model, so she was accustomed to being the centre of attention.

Sporting a black eye and a small facial cut, Tracie wept as she gave her account of the evening in question. It had begun as an 'ordinary night out'. She and her fiancé had shared a few drinks at the Marlbrook public house in Bromsgrove and then they had started out for their flat in nearby Alvechurch, Worcestershire. Not long into their drive Lee overtook a run-down Ford Sierra. The car he had passed was soon on his tail and the incident escalated to taunting, headlight flashing and a high-speed chase. At last, with his home in sight, Lee stopped. Both drivers got out of their vehicles and had a brief but fierce exchange. After the Sierra driver had returned to his car, his passenger then left the vehicle and attacked Lee. Tracie told the assembled reporters that she had confronted the man.

'I told him to F-off and he called me a slut and punched me. When I got up he was walking back to the car.'

The man, who had 'starey eyes' according to Tracie, was then driven away. Tracie attended to her fiancé, but she did not realize how serious his wounds were until a passing motorist approached with a flashlight.

'I tried to think of everything I should do,' she claimed to the press. 'I put my coat over him. I tried to stop the bleeding and comfort him.'

Tracie's story was horrifying, but it was by no means unique. Seven months earlier, a man had been stabbed to death at the side of the M25 after an argument with another driver. Several days after that, another man had been shot and killed while he was a passenger in a car that was travelling along a London street. The authorities decided that the cause of both murders was 'road rage'.

Tracie was admitted to hospital on the day after her emotional appearance at the news conference. Initial reports suggested that she had collapsed from strain, but it was later revealed that she had attempted suicide by taking a large dose of aspirin, tranquillizers and paracetamol. Even though she was the mother of a 5-year-old daughter, Tracie had left a suicide note in which she had written that she had nothing to live for – she only wanted to be with Lee. Then on 7 December, shortly after her release from hospital, Tracie was arrested. She collapsed and was taken back into medical care, where she remained under custody.

MOUNTING EVIDENCE

In the meantime, the police continued their investigation.

They descended on the small home that the couple had shared with two daughters from previous relationships. Roadblocks were set up and 650 motorists were interviewed in the search for the battered Ford Sierra. Dogs were then brought to the crime scene in the hope that they would be able to uncover the murder weapon. Tracie was still in police custody when, on 19 December, she was charged with murdering her fiancé.

The evidence that had been gathered by the police began appearing in the media. It appeared that Lee had been clutching a clump of Tracie's hair when he had died. A major inconsistency in the former model's story had also been found. She had told the police that the attack on Lee had occurred in front of his car, yet blood was found at the rear as well. Tracie was found to have had a history of violent behaviour. The 18-month relationship she had shared with her fiancé had been volatile and unstable and Lee had walked out on three separate occasions. The couple had even been seen arguing at the pub on their 'ordinary night out'. But Tracie stuck by everything that she had told the police. She even appealed for witnesses to come forward with information that would prove her innocence.

On 30 June 1997, Tracie's murder trial began at Birmingham Crown Court. The prosecution alleged that the argument that had begun in the Marlbrook public house had continued on the way home. At some point it had become so heated that Lee had stopped the car and both of them had got out. He was then stabbed 30 times – not 15, as the media had reported. Tracie had plunged a small, imitation Swiss Army knife into her fiancé's neck, face, head, chest, shoulder and back.

LANDSLIDE OF INFORMATION

The evidence that had been leaked to the media provoked a landslide of information.

Two witnesses said they had seen Lee's Ford Escort travelling back from the public house, but no car had been following. The motorist who had come across the murder scene testified that Tracie had not been tending to her injured fiancé, nor had she been trying to get help from a nearby house. Instead, she was found covered in blood, standing next to the car. She made no mention of the shabby Ford Sierra or the murderous man with 'starey eyes'. Another person who had come upon the bloody scene – coincidentally, a former police detective – testified that Tracie had been suspected from the start. The dead man's fiancée had not been able to recall the make, the colour or the licence plates of the other vehicle, yet by the time the police arrived she was able to provide a detailed description. Added to that, the pattern of bloodstains on Tracie's clothing was consistent with an attack, but inconsistent with the marks that would have been created when cradling a dying man. It was also suggested that an elongated blood-stain found on the lining of a boot Tracie had been wearing had been created when hiding the bloody knife. It was alleged that the weapon had been disposed of during her six visits to a private hospital lavatory.

Further evidence of a troubled relationship was presented. A policeman testified that on 19 October 1996 he had stopped Tracie as she was attempting to hit her fiancé. Just a few weeks later, Tracie had been seen biting and punching her fiancé in a nightclub. In neither case did Lee retaliate. He appeared to have been attempting to placate Tracie.

However, the defence put forward the possibility that Lee had been killed in a dispute over a drug deal. It was said that the dealer had followed Lee and Tracie out of the pub on the evening of the murder. The police were then accused of abandoning their hunt for the mysterious dark Sierra after only three days.

The defence described Tracie and Lee as a couple that 'had found glamour in each other, charm with each other'. Tracie's solicitor pointed out that she was wearing her engagement ring on the night of the murder, and had continued to wear it despite his death. 'She was committed to him,' he said. It was acknowledged that the relationship had been difficult at times, mainly because of an abortion. Tracie had recognized that adding a child to the relationship would have placed a further strain on a tenuous financial situation. The solicitor said that the abortion procedure had caused Tracie to lose her figure. Lee had made some unpleasant comments, but had later apologized and had paid for breast surgery.

Lee was presented as an immature, jealous man who could not accept his fiancée's past relationships. He was said to have hit Tracie 'once or twice'. Then a witness with a substantial criminal record was brought forward to testify that he had been threatened with a knife by the driver of a red Ford Granada three months before Lee's murder. Finally, the accused took the stand. Tracie denied that there had been any argument at the pub. She could not explain how her hair came to be found in the victim's hand, but added, 'My hair comes out easily anyway.' Tracie's solicitor had earlier suggested that the crime might have been racially motivated. Lee, who had dark skin, had been called a 'Paki bastard' by his killer, it was said. This theory was supported by Tracie.

THE JURY DECIDE

On 27 July 1997, the jury of nine women and three men began its deliberations. While they were awaiting the decision, Tracie and her family had what was described as a 'premature celebration' – a party held in her parents' garden. In the end, the former model had nothing to rejoice about. On 29 July, the jury found her guilty of murder. She was subsequently sentenced to life imprisonment, accompanied by the recommendation of a 14-year minimum term. In October 1998, Tracie failed in an attempt to appeal her conviction.

Six months later, the one-time model wrote a letter to a friend in which she confessed to murdering Lee. Published in the 18 April 1998 edition of the *News of the World*, the letter tells of a night that was vastly different from the one that Tracie had described under oath in court.

According to Tracie's letter she and Lee had argued over an ex-lover, Andrew Tilston, the father of her daughter, when they were in the pub. During the ride home, the row had intensified to such an extent that Tracie had asked her fiancé to stop the car. She told him that she would rather walk the rest of the way home. True to her word, she got out of the car and began to march along the road. However, she soon came across Lee's parked car. He had been waiting for her. When he told her to get into the car she refused. After telling him that their relationship was over, she demanded the keys to the flat. The argument then took a nasty turn when Lee accused his fiancée of sleeping around. Tracie countered by taunting him about Andrew Tilston. Lee then got out of the car and pulled out a knife. He grabbed her by the hair and said 'See if Andy wants to see you with a f***ed-up face'. During the ensuing struggle, Tracie wrote that she managed to bring Lee to the ground with her knee. The couple then wrestled until Tracie picked up the knife. Her letter continued,

*I must have stabbed him. Then he stood still and shouted, 'You f****** bitch,' then hit me so hard I fell again. I got up halfway and all I can remember is seeing red. I just went mad. Everything went like slow motion. I was shaking and had lost all control, all the abuse I had suffered and all the nasty things that had been thrown in my face, the way he had openly admitted to hating my relationship with my daughter and the fact that he had held the knife to me and was going to either slash my face or stab me, had just come to a head. I have never ever in my whole life lost control like I did this night.*

Much of the remainder of the letter described Tracie's rather weak attempt at covering her tracks. She revealed the fate of the missing knife – it had been flushed down the hospital lavatory. Then she claimed that she had thought about admitting her guilt after the failed suicide attempt, but, as she said in her letter,

> My family, Lee's family, were going through a nightmare. How could I be the one to say, 'This is what happened — Lee was either going to slash my face or stab me, but I got the knife and it was me who killed him'. Please God tell me, how do you ever come to terms with something like this?

And so, ultimately, Tracie's letter was an excuse – a means of communicating the claim that she had killed Lee in self-defence. 'Lee', she went on to say, 'was a Jekyll and Hyde character'. The *News of the World* declined to reveal how it had come by the letter and whether any payment was involved. In any case, the letter failed to reach its desired effect: most people believed only a fraction of what Tracie had claimed.

Throughout her incarceration, Tracie has proved to be a consistent source of fodder for the tabloids. She has become friends with Jane Andrews, the woman who was convicted of stabbing her boyfriend to death in 2001. Despite Tracie's insistence that she should now be referred to as 'Tia Carter', the media have dubbed the pair the 'Andrews Sisters'.

CELESTE BEARD
'Why doesn't he
die already?'

At 68 years of age and weighing 300 pounds Steven Beard might not have been the sort of man a 30-year-old, attractive blond woman like Celeste Johnson would have taken up with. Yet she eagerly entered his life. She would claim that she was motivated by love, but others saw her as a woman who was attracted to money – and Steven had lots of it.

The large Texan was a perfect example of the 'self-made man'. After working his way up from the lowest ranks in the radio business, he switched to television. Finally, he wound up as general manager and partner of one of the original affiliates of the FOX network in Austin. Celeste's achievements were nowhere near as impressive. Born in 1963, she was one of four children adopted by Edwin and

Nancy Johnson of Ventura County, California. She told her closest friends that her upbringing had been anything but pleasant. For a start, she said, her adoptive father had begun to sexually abuse her when she was four years old. This had been followed by similar treatment at the hands of an older adoptive brother. When she was 17 years old, Celeste had become pregnant. She married the father, gave birth to twin girls and then found herself stuck in a physically abusive marriage. In 1983, the couple divorced.

Other marriages followed. There was a US Air Force mechanic named Harold Wolf and a Mexican-American named Jimmy Martinez, but neither relationship was happy. It also seemed that Celeste could never get enough money. This hunger for riches led to a three-month prison sentence for insurance fraud after she had been caught burning a car she had reported stolen. She met Steven in 1993, when she was working as a waitress at the exclusive Austin Country Club in Austin, Texas. The television executive and his wife Elise spent a great deal of time at the club. They enjoyed eating, drinking and playing rounds of golf. But then Elise became ill. After being diagnosed with cancer she suffered a rapid decline and she died on 13 October 1993.

The 68-year-old widower and the 30-year-old waitress went out on their first date before Halloween. They soon became a couple. That Christmas, Steven gave his new sweetheart a $3,000 wristwatch, a $16,000 diamond cocktail ring and a brand new Ford Explorer SUV. Six days later, she moved into his spacious 5,300 square foot (492 square metres) mansion in Travis County, just west of Austin, Texas. After that, Steven started to clean up the financial and legal mess that Celeste had left behind her. He paid $20,000 in restitution for the insurance fraud and then he funded a custody battle that successfully wrested Celeste's twin girls away from their father's family. Along the way, the senior citizen sold his share of the television station, banking several million dollars in the process. Then he proposed. The couple married at the Austin Country Club on 18 February 1995, but not before a prenuptial agreement had been signed. Celeste would only be able to claim $500,000 in the event of a divorce.

AN UNEASY START

The marriage got off to an uneasy start. On the evening of their marriage, Steven had Celeste inject him with a drug that would enable him to maintain an erection. She found the process unpleasant and 'kind of traumatizing'. The sexual relationship, it seemed, had hit a wall. After four months of marriage, Steven filed for divorce, only to withdraw the petition after Celeste agreed to an oral sex session every Sunday morning. She made no secret of the arrangement. Her daughters and at least one of their boyfriends were told that she had to 'make some money'. But no amount of money could cover her reckless spending habits.

Celeste enjoyed a monthly allowance of $10,000, which she spent on clothing, shoes and expensive lunches. There were also parties – extravagant affairs that were thrown whenever Celeste got it into her mind to do so. At first, Steven appeared to take it all in his stride. He happily covered his wife's debts when she went beyond her allowance. However, as the marriage wore on and Steven's wealth diminished, the couple began to fight. At one point

Steven decided to give Celeste the $500,000 prenuptial payment right there and then. He thought that his wife would be more careful with money of her own. Perhaps she was – but the money was gone within six months.

Celeste's careless and carefree spending was only one aspect of her flawed personality. She began to openly refer to Steven as a 'fat f***' and she was even overheard expressing the wish that he would die. Worse than this, Celeste began spiking Steven's food and drink with sleeping pills so that she could slip out to meet one of her ex-husbands. Clearly she was spinning out of control. After Steven's accountant reported that she had spent something approaching $300,000 on Christmas shopping and entertaining, Steven told his wife that he was cancelling her credit cards. Celeste retaliated by threatening suicide. Faced with an intolerable and perhaps dangerous situation, Steven felt it best to check Celeste into St David's Pavilion, an expensive mental health facility in Austin.

She had been there no more than a few weeks when she met a 35-year-old woman named Tracey Tarlton, who was the manager of a chain bookstore in the centre of Austin. Tracey was the daughter of a lawyer, so her early days had been privileged. However, her later life had been troubled by a suicide attempt and battles with drugs and alcohol. Although she held a degree in biology from Texas A & M University, her original career path had been unfulfilling, so the bookstore job had been something of a godsend.

As a lesbian, Tracey was brought into contact with people who accepted and sometimes shared her sexual orientation. Along the way she had acquired a knowledge of books and publishing that was impressive enough to be recognized by the media, including the C-SPAN television network. She had been invited to appear on air on more than one occasion.

Tracey's much improved existence had been in danger of being destroyed in February 1999, when she had suffered a nervous breakdown. She had threatened customers and fellow employees and had screamed obscenities. However, she was fortunate enough to be supported by her family and friends, so she checked herself into St David's Pavilion.

Tracey made no attempt to hide her strong feelings for Celeste. She sent love letters to her within weeks of their first meeting. 'Celeste, you are so beautiful,' she wrote in one of them. 'I think about your long, silky body and your incredible, long legs and I just can't stand it.'

According to Tracey, the two women first had sexual relations on 20 March, just days after they first met. They were not terribly discreet it seems, because they were caught together by the staff at Timberland, a second mental institution to which they had both been transferred. The two women did not bother to hide their affection for each other after they were released. Celeste's daughters came upon the two women having sex on at least two occasions. When they confronted their mother, Celeste made light of the situation by saying, 'Tracey's a lesbian, and she's in love with me. Isn't it funny?'

A RUDE AWAKENING

Steven did not take the matter so lightly. On 29 September, after having spotted the pair kissing, he banished Tracey from the house. Three days later, he awoke at just before three in the morning to find his intestines exposed. Although he was clearly stupefied by the situation he suddenly found himself in, Steven had the presence of mind to reach for the telephone on his night table. He called 911 for help. The horror of the situation was captured on tape.

> Beard: 'I need an ambulance. My guts just jumped out of my stomach. They blew out – yeah, they blew out of my stomach. They're lying on my stomach.'
> 911 Operator: 'Okay. They're laying on your stomach?'
> Beard: 'I'm in awful pain.'
> 911 Operator: 'How did this happen?'
> Beard: 'It just happened. I woke up. I just woke up.'

As deputy sheriffs and an ambulance hurried to the scene the operator, Chandra Villegas, kept Steven on the line. 'I don't know what happened,' the dying man said. 'I've never had this happen before.' Again, he displayed a clear mind. He asked that his wife be called. After Steven hung up to free the line, the operator tried calling Celeste, who was supposedly sleeping in another room. But the phone just rang and rang. It seemed that Celeste just slept through it all. The deputies and the paramedics arrived to find the house locked. They ran around the outside of the house, peering through the windows. Then they spotted Steven lying on his blood-soaked bed. A patio door was shattered so that they could gain entry. Throughout all of this Celeste and one of her daughters remained asleep. They had to be woken by the police.

While the paramedics were working on Steven, they tried to find the cause of this life-threatening situation. Could it be that an incision from an operation had failed? The mystery was soon solved when one of the deputies found a freshly ejected shell casing from a 20-gauge shotgun lying on the bedroom floor. It was all too obvious that Beard required expert medical attention: he was taken by helicopter to Austin's Brackenridge Hospital, leaving Celeste to follow in a police car.

After arriving at the hospital, the small group was joined by the girls, their boyfriends and Paul Knight, the investigator assigned to the case. Knight first expressed his sympathy and then he asked them if they knew who might have committed the crime. One of the boyfriends thought the answer seemed obvious: 'That crazy Tracey'. He was not alone in his suspicions. Almost everyone shared the same view. There was one exception – Celeste.

Two days after the shooting, detectives interviewed the bookstore manager at her apartment. They came away with an expensive Italian 20-gauge shotgun, a gift from her father, that Tracey used for skeet-shooting. It came as little surprise when ballistics tests revealed that the shell found on Steven's bedroom floor had been fired by Tracey's shotgun. She was immediately arrested and charged with assault.

Why assault and not murder?

Because the 75-year-old Steven was miraculously still alive. Indeed, after surviving the shotgun blast and seven surgical operations he was even showing signs of recovery.

The fact that her husband had been shot had little effect on Celeste. In fact, now that Steven was firmly planted in Brackenridge Hospital, she was free to shop – and shop. Records indicate that Celeste spent over

$550,000 in the first two months after her husband was shot. As Celeste spent his money, Steven became stronger. On 21 January 2000, after nearly 16 weeks in hospital, he was at long last able to return home. He died four days later.

There was a funeral. And then Steven Beard's widow went back to shopping.

A year passed, during which the prosecutors tried to get Tracey to change her story. They were convinced that Celeste had been involved in the death of her husband and yet the lesbian skeet-shooter was saying nothing. The prosecutors finally recognized that their efforts were in vain. On 16 February 2001 they charged Tracey with murder. Then five months afterwards all hell broke loose. It seems that Tracey had been reading an Austin newspaper when she had spotted a small piece about Celeste. The woman with whom she had been so smitten had married a bartender and part-time musician.

An angry Tracey called a meeting with the team of prosecutors. She told them that she had shot Steven for Celeste. It was not the first attempt she had made on his life. Tracey revealed that she and Celeste had failed in an earlier attempt to poison the retired television executive. After first getting him to drink 190 proof alcohol they had then fed him a cocktail of drugs. But nothing had killed him. The shotgun seemed the only solution.

On the evening of the murder, Celeste had left a door unlocked so that Tracey could slip in and shoot her husband. The murderous wife had seen nothing. She had remained in her room, ignoring every sound – even the telephone call from the 911 operator. On 28 March 2002, Celeste was arrested and charged with the murder of her fourth husband. At the bail hearing, Celeste's lawyer revealed that 16 months after Steven's death her client had just $7,289 left from the one million dollars she had received from the sale of the Beard home. She had received no funds in Steven's will.

Celeste's trial began on 3 February 2003. Her lawyer tried to portray Tracey as a 'predatory, aggressive lesbian' – a psychotic woman who was delusional in her belief that the murder victim's wife was in love with her. Celeste, for her part, denied any sort of physical relationship with Tracey. It was a doomed strategy, one that was torpedoed by a dozen eyewitnesses, including Celeste's own daughters. Kristina testified that her mother was disgusted by Steven and would often comment 'Why doesn't he just die already?'

After 23 hours of deliberation, the jury handed down a guilty verdict. Celeste was given a life sentence. She will be eligible for parole in 2043, aged 80 years old. Tracey Tarlton received a 20-year sentence for the murder of Steven Beard. The former bookstore manager returned to prison believing that she and her victim were 'betrayed by the same woman'.

SUE BASSO
murder and the
Mickey Mouse figurine

Louis 'Buddy' Musso couldn't really pass for a cowboy, even when he was dressed in a Stetson hat, blue jeans, neckerchief and pointy-toed boots. Not surprising, really. The frail-looking 59-year-old man had spent nearly all of his life in New Jersey, thousands of miles from the Great Plains. He also had the mental age of an 8-year-old child.

Despite his challenges, he had once enjoyed a happy, successful marriage. However, in 1980 his wife had died of cancer. Buddy lived in sheltered accommodation after his wife's death, where he had plenty of friends. He had even more friends at the supermarket, where he worked as a packer. Yet he was still very lonely, because he yearned for female companionship.

Buddy first met 44-year-old Sue Basso, the woman he came to call 'my lady love', in the spring of 1997. They had both been attending a church bazaar not far from his home. Sue had come to New Jersey from her home in Jacinto City, Texas, which was a 12-minute drive away from downtown Houston. The morbidly obese Sue might not have been the sort of woman most men would have found appealing, but Buddy had always been drawn to anyone who would show an interest in him. And Sue was certainly interested. Her visit to New Jersey was only short but there was more than enough time for love to bloom.

By the summer of 1998, Buddy was making plans to live in Texas with his 'lady love'. The supermarket packer began shipping his modest possessions to Jacinto City. Then he cashed a social security cheque so that he could buy an inexpensive engagement ring for his Texas sweetheart. On 14 June, a little more than a year after he had first met, and last seen, his lady love, Buddy stepped on to a Greyhound bus bound for Houston. He was never heard from again.

It was 26 August before anyone had an inkling that

something was wrong. A man jogging through one of the less picturesque neighbourhoods of Galena Park, the community adjacent to Jacinto City, found Buddy's corpse. Lying in a ditch, it had not looked like much at all. It is quite possible that the body had already been seen by dozens of people, who had perhaps taken it for a bundle of discarded clothing, or an old blanket.

A LINGERING DEATH

However, the authorities were immediately aware that they were looking at a murder scene. According to a later version of the incident, the New Jersey supermarket packer had probably died as a result of a blow to the head. That simple statement does not properly convey the full horror of Buddy's horrible, lingering death. The autopsy report amounted to seven pages. It was dominated by a list of injuries: a fractured skull, a broken nose, 17 cuts to the head, 14 broken ribs, cuts and cigarette burns to the back and bruises to all parts of the body, including the genitals. These injuries had been inflicted over a period that could have been as long as several weeks.

At first, the police were unable to identify the body, because there was nothing to work with. The clothes found on Buddy's corpse were not those he had been wearing when he had been killed. Someone had dressed the body in clean clothing. Several hours after the unidentified body had been found, Sue Basso walked into a Houston police station. She told them that Buddy Musso, the man with whom she had been living, had disappeared. Sue's timing was such that Buddy's corpse was still in the ditch. She was brought to the scene with her 24-year-old son, James O'Malley, jun., so that she could identify the body. When Sue saw the bloody and beaten supermarket packer she broke down in a fit of sobbing and wailing. In stark contrast, James O'Malley, jun., was expressionless – he was neither upset nor surprised by the sight. When he was asked whether he knew what might have happened to Buddy, he replied, 'Yeah, we killed him'.

James O'Malley, jun., had no problem with sharing what he knew with the police. He began by telling the authorities that the New Jersey native had been killed at the Houston apartment of a woman named Bernice

Miller. Buddy's transgression, according to James, had been that he had accidentally broken a Mickey Mouse figurine. After having been forced to kneel for several days, Buddy was burned with cigarettes before being kicked and beaten.

After he died, his body was dumped in a bathtub filled with water, bleach and kitchen cleaner. Finally he was dressed and thrown into the ditch. James showed the police a dustbin into which Buddy's clothing, and the bloody towels used in the cleanup, had been tossed.

James O'Malley, jun., Sue Basso and Bernice Miller were all arrested. Bernice Miller's two children, Craig and Hope Ahrens, were also taken in, together with Hope's fiancé, Terence Singleton. But why had James O'Malley, jun., who had everything to hide, been so helpful to the police? The answer might have had something to do with his rich fantasy life. Always dressed in army fatigues, he somehow thought he was a special operations soldier. Like Buddy, James O'Malley, jun., had a limited mental capacity. In all likelihood he failed to grasp the true reason behind the murder. Buddy might have received a beating for having broken the Disney figurine, but he was killed for his insurance policy.

The motive for the murder became clear when the police went along to Sue Basso's house with a search warrant. It was a cramped and cluttered place filled with old electronic devices, record albums, books and magazines. The investigators found a number of incriminating documents among the papers that were strewn about. For instance, there was an application to make Sue the payee of Buddy's social security cheques. There was also a will that named Sue as the sole beneficiary. However, even though the year on the document was 1997, a computer in the house revealed that it had been composed a little more than a week before the murder. Finally, police discovered that a $15,000 life insurance policy had been taken out on Buddy. It had been witnessed by Sue Basso, the beneficiary, as well as three of the other people who had been charged with the murder.

Then the police found a scrawled note in the pocket of a pair of Buddy's trousers. He had been trying to get help from a friend in New Jersey. Further investigation uncovered the sad fact that Buddy had once turned down an offer of assistance from Bruce Byerly, a concerned neighbour. In the week before the murder, Byerly had noticed that the former supermarket packer had a black eye and numerous other wounds. When the neighbour offered to call the police, Buddy had reportedly pleaded with him: 'No, you call anybody and she'll beat me again.' Just days before the murder an assault had taken place on a vacant patch of ground, not far from Bernice's apartment. The responding officer caught Terence Singleton and James O'Malley, jun., in the act of forcing Buddy to take a military-style run. When asked about his visible wounds, Buddy said that he had been beaten up by three Hispanics.

Armed with the knowledge they had gained from searching her house, the prosecutors decided to single Sue Basso out. While they sought maximum prison sentences for her accomplices, the perceived mastermind would face the possibility of the death penalty. Her actions had long gone unnoticed by the authorities, but now she was receiving the attention she deserved.

A SORDID PAST

Sue Basso was not a Texan – she had been born in Schenectady, New York. One of eight children, she had experienced a troubled childhood, which had resulted in a stay at a Catholic reform school. She had been attractive as a young woman. When she had been in her early twenties she had married a marine named James Peek. Although the couple had two children together, Christianna and James, jun., their wedded life was otherwise far from conventional. They both engaged in extramarital flings, often with the other spouse waiting in an adjoining room. The family moved around the country until 1982, when James was arrested, charged and convicted of molesting his 9-year-old daughter. He served 11 months in a North Carolina prison, during which time the children were sent to foster homes. Though they were later sent to live with relatives, within a decade Christianna and James, jun., were again living with their parents, this time in Houston.

At that point, Sue decided to reinvent herself and the family. She left Sue Peek behind and became Sue O'Malley, an Irish-American in the most clichéd sense of the term. The O'Malley house was painted green and it was decorated with shamrocks, harps and leprechauns. Christianna and James, jun., continued to be abused in this new setting. Sue would have sex with her son – she called him 'Bozo the F*** Clown'. This unhealthy family dynamic was made even worse when in 1993 Sue hooked up with Carmine Basso, the owner of the security firm at which she was employed. It was not long before Carmine moved in with James, Christianna and James, jun. After a few months, James left the house and his wife to the security firm owner.

In October 1995, Sue abandoned her Irish-American fantasy for something much grander. When she placed a $1,372 engagement announcement in the Houston Chronicle she was no longer plain Sue. She was now Suzanne Margaret Anne Cassandra Lynn Theresa Marie Mary Veronica Sue Burns-Standlinslowski, heiress to a Canadian oil fortune. 'Miss Burns-Standlinslowski', according to the announcement, was a former nun who had worked with the less fortunate in upstate New York. She was highly educated and had been an award-winning gymnast. The groom, Carmine Joseph John Basso, was described as having received the Congressional Medal of Honor, in recognition of his service in Vietnam.

However, Sue and Carmine never married. How could they? Sue was still married to James. Still, this bothersome legal matter did not prevent her from adopting Carmine's surname. At about the time that Sue met Buddy at the fateful church bazaar, Carmine died. As thin as his partner was obese, the security firm owner had succumbed to a severe acid reflux, which had been complicated by malnourishment. The sudden death left Sue without a source of income – but Buddy would soon provide the solution to that problem.

Sue would be tried in the last of the five trials that stemmed from Buddy's murder. She sat in her prison cell awaiting her turn as one by one her fellow conspirators met with justice. Her son, James O'Malley, jun., provided the court with a detailed account of the abuse that Buddy had suffered. It included beatings and dunkings and being denied food and water and access to a toilet. James O'Malley, jun. was found guilty of capital murder.

His sentence was life imprisonment. Bernice Miller and her son Craig Ahrens both pleaded guilty after admitting that they had hit Buddy. Bernice was sentenced to 80 years in prison while Craig would serve 60 years. Terence Singleton, too, was found guilty of capital murder with life imprisonment. Hope Ahrens' trial resulted in a hung jury, an outcome that actually worked in the prosecution's favour. The accused woman could then be offered a plea bargain in exchange for her testimony against Sue.

In July 1999, the trial of Sue Basso finally began. Nearly two years had passed since her arrest. In that time, her appearance had changed dramatically. She had shed over 200 pounds (91 kilograms) and she now tipped the scales at a mere 140 pounds (63.5 kilograms). After claiming that she was suffering from a string of symptoms such as paralysis, chest pain and stomach pain, she entered the courtroom in a wheelchair. The defendant seemed to pay little attention to the proceedings. Hope Ahrens was now the star witness for the prosecution. First of all she testified that she had seen Sue beat Buddy with her fists and a vacuum-cleaner attachment. She went on to say that she had also seen Sue whipping the victim with a belt. Then she had jumped up and down on Buddy after he had fallen to the floor. Finally, she had encouraged her son to kick him with his steel-toed combat boots.

Anyone who had been following the parade of trials would not have been surprised when on 28 August 1999 Sue was found guilty of capital murder. After Christianna had told the court about the abuse she had suffered as a child, Sue was given the death sentence.

Having kept her part of the plea bargain arrangement, Hope received the lightest sentence of all. She was sentenced to just 20 years in prison. She is the only one out of the six murder accomplices who has a hope of seeing the outside world again.

BETTY BRODERICK
a woman
scorned

He was one of the most prominent attorneys in California and she was a devoted spouse. That is, until her husband no longer wanted her.

Betty Broderick was born Elizabeth Anne Bisceglia on 7 November 1947. She had a middle class upbringing in Eastchester, New York, a quiet little town some 18 miles (30 kilometres) north of Manhattan. Her childhood was uneventful. It centred around a stable home life and the local Catholic church. After graduating from high school, Betty attended the College of Mount Saint Vincent, a Catholic liberal arts college. At that time it was devoted exclusively to the education of women.

Betty was 17 when she met Daniel T. Broderick III, her future husband, during a football game at the University of Notre Dame. It was the first out-of-town trip that Betty's parents had permitted her to take and it proved to be quite eventful. She fell immediately for the tall, lanky medical student. Betty and Dan dated for three years and in that time she often visited Dan's large Irish-American family in Pittsburgh. Dan spent a great deal of time on the road during the couple's courtship. He constantly travelled between Cornell Medical School, where he was completing his studies, and Betty's Eastchester home.

On 12 April 1969, Betty and Dan were married. The elaborate ceremony was organized by the bride's mother, after which the newlyweds honeymooned in the Caribbean. When they returned from honeymoon they set up home together in New York. It was the first time Betty had ever lived outside her parents' house. She became pregnant early in the marriage – during the honeymoon, in fact. In January of 1970, she gave birth to a daughter, Kimberly. Four more children followed in quick succession, including a baby boy who lived for just four days.

For many years, the couple lived a very modest lifestyle, which was a reflection of their day-to-day financial challenges. Although Dan completed his medical degree in 1970, he decided that he did not want to further his medical training. Instead, the young father enrolled in Harvard Law School, which enabled him to become an attorney. Betty worked hard to maintain the home throughout Dan's studies. As well as caring for the children, she brought in as much money as she could by selling Avon and Tupperware products on door to door. When Dan graduated in 1973, the family moved to San Diego. Dan used his knowledge of medicine to good effect by becoming a specialist in the field of medical malpractice. Courted by several law firms, he accepted a position as a junior partner with the firm Cary, Gray. Gradually, the Brodericks left their modest lifestyle behind. The couple were able to buy their first home, a spacious house in the city's Coral Reef neighbourhood.

While Dan was not yet making great amounts of money, it was all a vast improvement on the couple's previous lifestyle. However, he was devoting a considerable portion of the increased family income to his wardrobe and evenings out on the town with his fellow attorneys

- necessary expenses, he explained, if one wanted to get ahead. Meanwhile, Betty was still working very hard. She had moved on from selling cosmetics and kitchenware to teaching religious classes at a local Catholic school. Then in 1979 she earned her real estate licence, an accomplishment that came hot on the heels of Dan's departure from Cary, Gray. His aim was to create a law practice of his own – and he succeeded. Before long he was earning considerable sums of money.

Having finally achieved the status he had been seeking, Dan all but ended the late night outings with the other attorneys. There were still late nights, but these were limited to working at his office. The money began to accumulate. A maid was hired for the Broderick house and family vacations were grander and more frequent. However, as before, Dan seemed to want to spend most of his money on his own vanity. His expensive wardrobe was supplemented by contact lenses and a nose job.

THE OTHER WOMAN

Dan might have cut down on his socializing with other

lawyers, but it was through another law office that he met a beautiful, blond 21-year-old receptionist named Linda Kolkena. Although she was unable to type, and had nothing more than a high school education, Linda was hired by Dan as his personal assistant. It all looked quite suspicious to Betty but she held her tongue. She did not want to rock the marital boat when she had no proof that anything was going on. Meanwhile, Dan displayed little caution with regard to Linda. While on a trip with Betty to New York, the attorney was caught making a telephone call to her. And when the Brodericks were off on a family vacation to England, Dan had flowers wired to her.

The time finally came when Betty could no longer fool herself about what she was witnessing. She threw caution to the wind and telephoned one of Dan's female employees to ask if anything was going on between her husband and Linda. But she had chosen the wrong person. Not wanting to get involved, the woman denied any knowledge of what had become a very obvious affair. The employee would later tell Dan about the phone call. She was then summarily dismissed. Having been told that there was nothing going on, Betty's next move was to seek therapy. If her suspicions were unfounded, she thought, she must be suffering from some form of paranoia.

Betty's visits to the therapist continued until 22 November 1983, the date of Dan's 39th birthday. Carrying a dozen red roses and a bottle of champagne, she showed up unannounced at her husband's workplace. But what was meant as a pleasant surprise turned into one of the worst events of Betty's life. Dan was not at the office, though there were signs that he had been there earlier in the day. His desk was covered in cake crumbs and there were balloons and empty wine bottles strewn around the room. Linda was not at the office either. Dan's secretary told Betty that she had no idea where her husband was or when he would be returning. As she waited, it became clear to Betty that neither her husband nor his personal secretary would be coming back to the office that day.

SEEING RED

Eventually, Betty went home. Then, with her children watching, she pulled Dan's clothes out of his wardrobe and ripped them up. Finally, she made a bonfire of them in the back garden. Even after seeing the destruction, Dan said very little when he got home.

In a calm, seemingly rational, voice he told his wife that she had been imagining things. It was a variation on a speech that he had made on several previous occasions – whenever, in fact, he had been caught doing something suspicious. However, Dan's words were no longer effective. He had pushed Betty to a point where she could no longer fool herself into believing that her husband was faithful.

Dan continued his pretence for months. He denied all accusations and he played the innocent. It was not until 29 February – that most unusual of days – that he owned up to the affair. He did so out of necessity – he was seeking a legal separation from his wife.

This momentous announcement was not the only thing to disrupt the lives of the Broderick family. Weeks earlier, a crack had been discovered in the foundations of their Coral Reef home. Dan, Betty and the children had been forced to move to nearby La Jolia while the damage was being repaired. When the work was finished it was Dan who returned to the family home: Betty and the children remained at the rental house.

The separated husband immediately set out to create a new life for himself. First of all he redecorated the Coral Reef house. The message was clear – Betty could no longer call the house her own, even though she had done so much to make it into a home. She would, however, still visit it when she picked her children up, or dropped them off. It was during one such visit that Betty began committing ill-advised acts of vengeance. She once took a Boston cream pie from the kitchen that had once been hers and smeared it over Dan's bed and clothing. In reaction, the attorney took out a restraining order. He wanted to make sure that his estranged wife would no longer be able to set foot on the property. However, it was all in vain. Two days later, the tranquillity of the house was broken when Betty threw a wine bottle through his window.

By this point, it was quite clear that Betty needed the services of a good attorney. Her problem was that Dan was either a friend or an acquaintance of every one of San Diego's best divorce lawyers. Her first choice, a man named Thomas Ashworth, declined to take the case on, only to represent Dan in the early stages of the proceedings. Betty then looked to Los Angeles, two hours up the Pacific Coast, for a lawyer who would be willing to represent her. The attorney she found, Daniel Jaffe, advised Betty that her aggressive behaviour would count against her. Yet Betty's vandalism of the Coral Reef house continued. Worse still, Betty had taken to insulting Dan in front of their children and, it seemed, any neighbour within earshot. Despite her lawyer's advice, Betty's actions only seemed to become more serious. Things came to something of a head when she learned that Dan and Linda would be out of town. Grasping the opportunity, she broke into the house and smashed yet another window with yet another bottle.

ESCALATING AGGRESSION

By this time Dan had lost patience with Betty. He filed an Order to Show Cause, a document that required Betty to defend every one of her actions against a charge of contempt of court. And the list was getting longer by the day. It included spray painted walls, a smashed answering machine and broken doors. Instead of working towards a just settlement for his client, Betty's lawyer was forced to spend his time keeping his client out of jail.

Betty's actions during the Christmas season of 1985 posed yet another challenge. While Dan and Linda were holidaying with the Broderick children, Betty had once again broken into the Coral Reef house. She had ripped open gifts that had been meant for Linda and had smashed a large mirror. The break-in was just one of many factors that convinced Dan to sell the Coral Reef home. Instead, he moved into a pillared mansion in Balboa Park, the most beautiful neighbourhood in San Diego. Despite Betty's objections, the house in Coral Reef was disposed of. She retaliated by driving her Chevrolet van into the front of Dan's new home. After the police arrived, Betty was placed in a straightjacket and taken to a local mental hospital, where she spent three days.

Day and night, Betty would leave obscene telephone messages on Dan's Balboa Park answering machine.

They were often overheard by her children.

> *This is a message to f***head and the bitch. You have one hell of a nerve dumping the kids here on the sidewalk and zooming away without making any attempt to communicate with me about my plans for the weekend. Make me sick, both of you. I have a good mind to dump the kids back on you and drive away. Call me. We have a lot to talk about, asshole. And come pick up your four children that you're working so hard to have custody of. Congratulations. You can have them.*

The trail of destruction continued for years. It led to countless appearances before a number of judges and Betty was twice jailed for contempt of court. Nearly six years elapsed between the separation and the divorce trial. Then on 30 January 1989, after eight days spent in a courtroom, Dan and Betty's marriage was at long last dissolved. Though Betty had sought custody of the children, this was awarded to Dan. One mental health expert judged her unstable.

After assessing the couple's financial situation the presiding judge determined that Betty actually owed her husband $750,000, because of the cash advances that he had made during the previous six years. As a result, Betty received a total cash payout of just $30,000 after nearly 20 years of marriage. The divorce ended nothing. Betty's abuse and vandalism continued into the autumn of 1989. Then, in the early hours of 5 November, one last act brought it all to an end.

After dropping a recently purchased .38 calibre Smith & Wesson into her handbag, Betty left the cramped apartment in which she had been living since the divorce. She then drove to Dan's home and entered the house by using a key that she had stolen from one of her daughters several months earlier. It did not take long to find the master bedroom. Dan and Linda, newly married, were asleep when Betty fired the first shot. Linda flinched, but made no sound. She was then shot a second time. Dan awoke to see his ex-wife standing before him with a gun in her hand. When he tried to get out of bed, the attorney was shot in the back. He began coughing blood, which made him gradually choke to death. That afternoon, accompanied by an attorney, Betty surrendered herself to the San Diego police.

Her trial began on 22 October 1990, a little less than a year after the murders. It was a media sensation. Betty's counsel attempted to paint her as a woman who had simply snapped after being forced to endure a barrage of legal documents from her ex-husband. However, this line of defence became invalid in the face of the accused woman's answering machine messages, together with some very troubling testimony from witnesses. The dead man's housekeeper told the court that Betty had once stated that she would 'put four bullets in Dan's head, one for each of his children'. When Betty's children took the stand her defence was all but demolished. Her daughters – including Kimberly, who had been estranged from her father – testified that their mother had repeatedly stated her desire to kill Dan.

Needless to say, Betty's own account was somewhat different. The jury heard a story of her ex-husband's deceit and betrayal. While she remembered very little about the morning of the murder, she did recall a time when she had considered putting the gun to her own head in front of Dan and his new wife. But she had not proceeded with that plan of action, of course. All she could remember about what had actually taken place was contained within two brief sentences: 'I pushed the door open. They moved, I moved, and it was over.' After four days' deliberation, the jury returned to the courtroom. It had been unable to reach a verdict.

In October 1991 Betty returned to court for her second trial. It went much the same way as the first – with one dramatic difference. In the middle of the trial Betty's lawyer suggested that Dan might have tried to arrange for Betty's murder at some point. Any discussion of this theory was squashed by the court. At that point the defence appeared to lose direction.

Betty was eventually found guilty of murder in the second degree. She received two consecutive sentences of 15 years to life for the murders of Dan and Linda. In 2010 she was denied parole.

JOYCE COHEN
a murder paid in
cocaine

Stanley Alan Cohen did not have an enviable track record when it came to marriage. His first marriage had been blessed with two children, but it had ended in divorce. Before he had reached the age of 40, two other marriages had come and gone. In 1974 he was engaged to a fourth woman when he met a 24-year-old separated single mother named Joyce Lemay. His fourth fiancée would be forgotten – Joyce would become the next Mrs Cohen. She would also be the final Mrs Cohen – Joyce would make certain of that.

Born in 1934, Stanley Cohen spent his early years on Long Island before his father, a furrier, moved the family to Florida. Stanley adapted well to the change. He graduated from high school and then attended the University of Florida, where he gained a degree in civil engineering. A management position with a local construction firm followed. Then in 1963 Stanley established his own business, the SAC Construction Company. The name of the company was derived from his initials. His timing could not have been better. Florida's population doubled in the two decades that followed and SAC Construction was awarded contracts to build government offices, warehouses, shopping plazas and medical facilities. Before long, Stanley began funding real estate development from the profits that streamed into his construction company. It seemed that nothing he touched was anything less than a great success – except, that is, his marriages.

Joyce Lemay's life had followed a totally different course. Born in 1951, her home town was Carpentersville, Illinois, a small city about an hour outside Chicago. Both of her parents drank, which led them into a steady stream of low-paying jobs and nagging financial problems. Much of her life had been spent in the rural south, where her father had gone to seek work as a sharecropper.

The relocation did nothing to strengthen the family and Joyce's parents soon split up. Joyce lived with her mother for a time before being shipped off to a number of orphanages, foster homes and youth facilities.

Things took a turn for the better when she reached the age of 13. She was given a home by an aunt. However, this relatively calm period came to an end four years later, when Joyce married a drywall installer named George McDillon.

The young newlyweds were soon joined by a son, who was christened Shawn. After the birth of their son the couple bought a small house and worked hard to support their modest lifestyle. It is likely that they would have succeeded if Joyce had not begun living beyond their means. Then in 1973, five years into their struggle, Joyce convinced George to relocate the family to Florida. He found work not far from Fort Lauderdale, in the city of Coral Springs. But George quickly realized that Joyce would never be satisfied with being the wife of a man who could only command a modest income. Within twelve months, he had returned to Illinois.

A WHIRLWIND AFFAIR

Joyce was now a separated single mother. She met Stanley while she was working as a secretary at one of his offices. It could not have been said that she was a statuesque woman – she was only 5 feet (1.5 metres) tall – but she was striking. The couple began a whirlwind affair which left everyone shaking their heads. Within weeks of meeting Joyce, Stanley traded one fiancée for another. For her part, Joyce worked hard at bringing an official end to her marriage to George. On 5 December 1974, ten days after her divorce became final, Stan married Joyce in an extravagant ceremony at the famous Dunes Hotel in Las Vegas.

The newlyweds lived at their Miami home for much of the year. It was a beautiful old mansion that overlooked Biscayne Bay. The winter months were spent at their 650-acre ranch, just outside the Colorado city of Steamboat Springs, some 168 miles (270 kilometres) northwest of Denver. Steamboat Springs is known as 'Ski Town USA'. It was a privileged life, complete with servants, fine furnishings, designer labels and cocaine... plenty of cocaine.

Of course, Joyce was no longer expected to work as a secretary. Stan paid for her education at a local school of interior design and made sure that his company supplied her with clients – but she much preferred shopping to work. 'Your mother's going to shop me to death', Stan had once joked to Shawn.

And yet despite Joyce's expensive tastes and her penchant for spending money, Stan just grew richer and richer. But even though the Cohens' fortunes had reached new heights by the 1980s, their marriage had begun to go in the opposite direction. Joyce had discovered that Stan had been having an affair with an old girlfriend. When she threatened to leave her husband, he countered by saying that she would receive nothing – she would return to the lifestyle of a humble secretary.

Frustrated and angry, Joyce told a friend that she wished Stan were dead. Others had heard her mention the possibility of hiring a hit man.

Joyce became reckless in other ways. Her liking for cocaine became an addiction – she snorted it at the ranch, in her mansion and during wild evenings at the

Champagne Room, her favourite Miami nightclub. When Shawn also developed a drug problem she had him shipped off to a boarding school, where he could be taught discipline and self-control. The absurdity of this decision never occurred to her.

All the years of unhappiness came to a sudden, jarring end on the morning of 7 March 1986. At 5.25am, Miami 911 received a hysterical call from Joyce – she told them that her husband had been shot in the head. As the police raced to respond, Joyce stayed on the line. She explained to the operator that she had been working through the night on a charity project while her husband had been asleep in their upstairs bedroom. After hearing a gunshot, Joyce had spotted two figures fleeing the mansion.

As soon as they arrived at the scene, the police could see that they were facing an unorthodox homicide investigation. Stanley Cohen had been one of Miami's most successful developers – had been, because the man was most definitely dead. The case became even more unusual when Joyce ordered the police to leave the mansion. They had only been there for an hour. That was not the sort of thing they expected to hear from a woman whose husband had just been murdered.

Eight hours passed before the authorities managed to return with a search warrant. They soon located the murder weapon. Stanley had been shot with his own Smith & Wesson revolver. The gun was hidden amongst some ferns in the garden. Joyce told the police that her husband had last carried the gun about five hours before his death, when she had asked him to investigate some noises coming from outside the house. It was her theory that he had left the gun on his night table instead of putting it away. She suggested that the intruders had then used the firearm to murder her husband.

Joyce's unlikely story became more difficult to believe as the detectives set about their work. While they were combing the Cohen mansion they found a tissue that bore traces of gunpowder and mucous. A forensic examination of the item revealed that it had come from Joyce. Then there was the witness who said that he had heard the sound of gunshots at three o'clock in the morning, which was the very time of death that had been fixed by the medical examiner. It appeared that Joyce had waited over two hours before telephoning 911.

As far as Stanley's children were concerned the mystery had been solved. They filed a five million dollar wrongful death lawsuit against their stepmother and then they took steps to prevent her from gaining access to the estate. Joyce countered by suing her stepchildren for slander. And yet she still had not been charged. Faced with a high profile lawyer hired by Joyce, the authorities wanted to make certain that all of the evidence was in place before they arrested the widow.

POLICE BREAKTHROUGH

Then there was a breakthrough. As the detectives worked on the case they were contacted by a lawyer representing a prisoner named Frank Zuccarello, who had been arrested four days after Stanley's murder. Zuccarello was a thief who specialized in high-value burglary. He told the police that Joyce had hired him, along with two other men, to kill her husband. According to Zuccarello, the former secretary gave Stan's gun to the trio, along with a detailed sketch of the mansion. She then locked up her pet Doberman and shut off the alarm system. Finally, she made sure that a door was left unlocked. Zuccarello and his accomplices had received $100,000 worth of cocaine for their services.

Joyce was arrested on 2 November 1988. Over two years had passed since Stanley's murder. Things had changed radically for the widow. Instead of living in one of Miami's most valuable homes she had moved to a Virginia trailer park with a new boyfriend.

When Joyce came to trial a large number of witnesses queued up to testify against her. Among them was country singer Tanya Tucker, who spoke of Joyce's obvious dissatisfaction with the marriage. Then a construction worker with whom she had snorted cocaine took the stand. He described a conversation in which Joyce had said that she wished she could find someone to kill Stan. When Zuccarello took the stand he was challenged by Joyce's lawyer, who argued that the thief had fabricated a story about a contract killing in order to get out of prison. The jury was having none of it. At the end of the three week trial it delivered a guilty verdict. Joyce was subsequently sentenced to life imprisonment, with a further 15 years for conspiring to kill her husband.

'You committed the crime for financial gain,' summed up the presiding judge, Fredricka Smith, 'and you did it in a cold, calculating manner.'

Of course, Joyce received no money from Stanley's estate. Her son, Shawn, received a $106,000 inheritance but he spent it all on drugs.

ADELE CRAVEN
Do you guys know where I can hire
a hit man?'

Stephen Craven was a good family man. Many people viewed him as a role model.

On Sunday mornings he and his wife Adele could be found welcoming the faithful at the Vineyard Christian Church. The couple met in California when Stephen was serving as a pilot with the United States Coast Guard. They married in 1989. Three years later they moved to Edgewood, Kentucky, just south of Cincinnati, Ohio. In the intervening years Stephen had moved on from the Coast Guard. He was now employed as a pilot by Delta Air Lines. Adele had adopted the role of stay-at-home mother, so that she could raise the couple's two sons. Otherwise she was a licensed mortician.

The relationship looked ideal. However, as with so many

marriages, outward appearances could be deceptive. Not that there appeared to be any major problems. According to Adele, Stephen would complain about her weight and spending habits while she found him inflexible. But Stephen was making an effort to change his ways. He had sought counselling to improve their family life. His goals were recorded in a binder kept in their home. Beside 'Husband' he had written:

Lift up and compliment Adele. Her love and partnership make her the most important person in my life. Encourage her growth and independence. Provide Adele the security of unconditional love. Always be courteous and seek her wise counsel. Engage Adele in every level of planning.

What Stephen did not know, though, was that Adele was no longer interested in the marriage – she had found another man. He was red-headed Russell 'Rusty' McIntire, a 32-year-old baggage handler with Delta Air Lines. Rusty was married with children. He supplemented his modest salary by working as a handyman. Rusty and Adele met in the spring of 2000, after he was hired to remodel the basement of the Craven house. It wasn't long before the relationship between the housewife and the handyman became sexual. On the first day of June they were caught having sex in the parking lot of St Pius X Catholic Church, not far from Rusty's Erlanger, Kentucky home. By this time, Adele and Rusty had already begun discussing ways in which Stephen might be killed. Bike trails, his boat and the house were all considered as possible murder sites.

A NEW FRIEND

Incredibly, Stephen thought he had found a new friend in Rusty. The two men spent time together, including a boating excursion that took place on 8 June. The very next day, Rusty and Adele met up with Ronald Scott Pryor, a 33-year-old car washer at an Erlanger bowling alley. Although they hoped Pryor would murder Stephen, it took a few days to bring him around to the idea. Pryor finally accepted the job during a telephone conversation with Adele on 11 June, in which she offered to pay him $15,000 for the killing. The next morning, the 38-year-old pilot was beaten and shot to death in the very basement that he had hired Rusty to renovate.

Adele told the police that she and her children had arrived home from shopping to find the house unlocked. She had called for help after coming across her husband's bludgeoned body lying face down in the basement. Detectives worked at impressive speed to solve the case, but there was never much doubt that Adele was involved in the murder. She was arrested and charged nine days after the event. On 28 July, Rusty was also arrested and charged with murder. Pryor remained at liberty for another day, but he too was then apprehended.

In spite of the speed at which the detectives had worked, Adele's case did not come to court until 28 October 2002. Much had happened in the 27 months since she had been arrested. In a separate trial, Pryor had already been found guilty of murdering Stephen. The jury had recommended that he should receive the death penalty. Worse still, Rusty had pleaded guilty to his part in the crime. What is more, he had agreed to testify against his former lover in order to avoid the death penalty. Rusty was now the prosecution's star witness.

A DAMNING ACCOUNT

The prosecution opened its case against Adele by painting the most gruesome picture of Stephen Craven's final moments. Adele had lured Stephen into the basement by telling him that the family's pet ferret had escaped its cage. When he went to investigate Pryor leapt out from behind a couch, crowbar in hand. The contracted killer delivered a blow that knocked Stephen to the floor. As he lay there the beating continued. But despite receiving twelve blows to the head with the crowbar, he did not die. When Adele saw that Stephen was still alive she produced her husband's .38 calibre revolver and ordered Pryor to shoot him with it. A bullet was fired into Stephen's brain – and still the pilot did not die. Adele reloaded the gun, gave it back to the hit man and told him to fire another two shots into Stephen's body.

The prosecution claimed that Adele had wanted to be rid of her husband. At first, she had hoped that he might die in a plane crash, so that she could benefit from his $500,000 life insurance policy. But she seemed to have realized that having her husband killed would achieve the same purpose. On the other hand, the defence put forward a scenario in which hiring Pryor had been Rusty's idea alone. Adele had nothing whatsoever to do with the killing, it was argued. The baggage handler was portrayed as a heavy drinker who had become obsessed with the airline pilot's wife. Rusty had stalked her, spied on her and eventually seduced her. Then when Adele had decided to end the relationship, he had hired a hit man to kill Stephen. He saw him as a rival for her affections.

Adele took the stand in her own defence. Her testimony lasted for a total of 14 hours, spread over two days. She acknowledged that her marriage had not been a perfect one, but she had loved Stephen – there was no way she would ever kill her husband.

'Rusty implicated me to save his own skin,' she said. 'He is betraying me.'

The accused woman did not deny that she had talked to her neighbours about hiring a hit man to kill her husband, but said it had been nothing more than a joke.

'I said, "Do you guys know where I can hire a hit man?" They laughed. I said, "No, Steve really pissed me off." It became a joke after that. I know I said it at least one more time out of anger. I never meant it. I never meant it.'

On 4 December, the state prosecutors and the defence took ten hours to make their closing arguments. After being sequestered for the evening, the jury began their deliberations on 5 December. On the following day they returned to the courtroom. The foreman of the jury announced that they could not reach a verdict. Eight jury members wanted to find Adele 'not guilty', while three others thought that she should receive the death sentence sought by the state. The final jury member was unable to come to a conclusion at all.

A second trial began on 12 January 2004, in Lexington. But this time there was a significant difference – the hit man had agreed to speak in order to avoid a death sentence. Pryor's testimony was detailed, damning and convincing and it supported the prosecution in every way. Faced with this testimony, Adele saw only one way out. Some days later she pleaded guilty to one count of complicity to murder. The pilot's wife received a life sentence but she will be eligible for parole in 2024.

EVELYN DICK

'How could you, Mrs Dick?'

Canadians of a certain age will remember a rather rude, though clever, school playground rhyme.

You cut off his legs.
You cut off his arms.
You cut off his head.
How could you, Mrs Dick?

Mrs Evelyn Dick, formerly Evelyn MacLean, was a dark-eyed beauty who came to prominence when the body of her husband, John, was discovered on a pleasant spring morning in 1946. An unusual feature of the case was the fact that his head, arms and legs were missing.

Evelyn MacLean was born on 13 October 1920 in Beamsville, a small Ontario town situated just south of Lake Ontario. In the following year, her father, Donald, found work as a streetcar conductor, so he moved the family some 25 miles (40 kilometres) west to Hamilton. By all accounts, Donald MacLean was not a pleasant man. As well as being a drinker he was foul-tempered and unfriendly, to the point that he insisted that Evelyn be kept apart from the other children in the neighbourhood. And yet none of this behaviour hindered Donald's advancement within the Hamilton Street Railway Company. He was soon promoted to an office job. There was, of course, an increase in salary, but this does not account for the fairly lavish lifestyle that the MacLean family came to enjoy. An explanation of sorts can be gleaned from the fact that young Evelyn was sent shopping with a purse full of nickels – the standard streetcar fare. As Evelyn entered womanhood, her visits to the shops were punctuated by the extravagant parties she hosted at the Royal Connaught Hotel and other glitzy venues. Clothed in expensive dresses, jewellery and furs, she began to be seen in the company of any number of wealthy older men.

Evelyn provided a lot of grist for Hamilton's well-oiled rumour mill. However, the town gossips must surely have viewed 1942 as a very special year indeed. First, it seemed that the attractive 21-year-old girl was losing her figure. Then it was announced that she was pregnant. According to Evelyn the father of her child was her husband, a navy man named Norman White who was serving overseas. It seemed that none of the gossipers had picked up on the marriage – and no one knew of any Mr White.

Evelyn's mysterious husband was not even present on 10 June 1942, when she gave birth to a daughter, Heather Maria White. Sadly, the child was mentally retarded. Evelyn's second pregnancy, in 1943, was even more troublesome. This time she gave birth to a stillborn child. Before the end of the year she was again pregnant, and on 5 September 1944 she gave birth to Peter David White, a seemingly healthy boy. Again the elusive Mr White was nowhere in sight. Perhaps he was still serving overseas? But then how could Evelyn's pregnancies be explained?

The rumour mill turned even more quickly when it became known that Evelyn was no longer Mrs White. On 4 October 1945 she married John Dick, a 39-year-old Russian motorman with the Hamilton Street Railway. The wedding came just weeks before the birth of young Peter. Not that the newlyweds were actually living together, mind you – the bride remained in a downtown apartment that she shared with her now-separated mother. Evelyn's supposed second marriage was several weeks old when she joined her new husband at a house she had bought on Carrick Avenue. Where the young, unemployed woman got the money for the purchase has always been a source of mystery. John would not have been able to provide much of anything and his name is absent from the mortgage. And yet somehow Evelyn thought that the Hamilton Street Railway employee had a reasonable amount of money. She hoped that he would be able to enrich her lifestyle and help her to achieve a higher social standing.

AN ABRUPT END

Whatever the relationship between John and Evelyn

Dick, it came to an abrupt end in a matter of months. In early February 1946 the groom moved in with his cousin, Alexander Kammerer. The arrangement seemed to be working well enough, but on the afternoon of 6 March John Dick disappeared. On the following day some workmen found John's shirt. It was bloody and buttoned up and the sleeves had been cut off. Although the Hamilton Police Department suspected foul play, they also wondered whether the missing man, despite his honest reputation, might not have run away from a problem. On 12 March, they received a phone call from an anonymous female who asked whether John Dick had been arrested for 'Running away with money and tickets belonging to the company – the Hamilton Street Railway'.

Four days later, John's torso was discovered by five children who had been playing on the Niagara Escarpment, a majestic formation that bisects the city of Hamilton. At first, the small group thought they had found a headless pig, but when they poked at it with sticks they realized in horror that the carcass was human. The police assumed that the children's imaginations must have been working overtime, so they were reluctant to investigate. However, the juvenile sleuths were soon to be proved right. They had, indeed, stumbled upon a torso. A casual inspection revealed bullet holes and a wound that was deep enough to suggest that an attempt had been made to cut the remains in two. The surrounding area was sealed off immediately and a fruitless search for the head, arms and legs was undertaken.

Word of the shocking discovery moved quickly among the citizens of Hamilton. The missing man's brother-in-law was soon contacted. Although there was little to see, he did not hesitate to confirm that the torso was John's.

'Don't look at me. I don't know anything about it,' Evelyn said, when she was informed about her husband's shocking death.

And yet despite having denied any knowledge she quickly launched into a story about a well-dressed, though rough-looking, Italian who had arrived at the Carrick Avenue house in search of John. According to Evelyn, the man was in a rage after discovering that her husband had been fooling around with his wife. She told the police that the anonymous man had threatened to 'fix' the Russian motorman.

WEB OF LIES

A far more valuable piece of information surfaced a few days later. The police learned that on the afternoon of 6 March, at around the time of John's disappearance, Evelyn had borrowed a car from a man named William Landeg. She had later returned it with one of the front seats covered in blood. What is more, the seat covers were missing and the boot of the car contained two blood-covered items: a sweater and a tie. Evelyn's story was that Heather had cut her face and had been taken to the hospital for stitches.

When the police discovered that the blood found in the car matched John's, Evelyn came out with yet another tale. According to her revised account, she had received a telephone call from a second anonymous man, who had told her that John had impregnated his wife. The caller added that he needed to borrow a car. Faced with this situation, Evelyn had turned to William Landeg for assistance. She had then met the mysterious man, who had been carrying a large sack that contained 'part of John' – or so she was told. Together they had driven up to the escarpment, where the torso was then dumped.

Even though Evelyn protested her innocence, she was taken into custody. The widow then produced yet another explanation. This one involved an Italian hit man hired by a man named Bill Bohozuk. As part of the investigation, the police began combing through the Carrick Avenue house for evidence. There was plenty to be found. A pair of bloodstained ladies' rubber boots was unearthed, as well as a quantity of ashes that contained traces of a human skull. When they went up to the attic, they found an old beige suitcase filled with cement. The police had not stumbled on John Dick's remains, though. When the block of cement was broken open the tiny body of Peter David White emerged. He had a cord around his neck and he was wrapped in a Red Cross nurse's uniform that had belonged to Evelyn.

Ever resourceful, Evelyn came up with one more excuse. Bill Bohozuk had killed her baby and her estranged husband. Most people would not know anything about Bill Bohozuk, who had come to figure so prominently in Evelyn's stories. To the Hamilton police, however, he was a well known figure in the city's underworld. As it turned out, 47-year-old Bohozuk was Evelyn's long-time lover. Quite possibly he was also the father of at least one of the 'White' children. Evelyn continued to come up with stories in which various criminals had been cruising the city streets in the hope of abducting and killing her husband, but the Hamilton Police Department had long since stopped believing the widow. They continued their investigation.

One lead was provided by Evelyn's mother, who told them that she had seen her estranged husband with the beige suitcase on the day before its discovery. A subsequent search of Donald MacLean's house revealed more bone and ashes, a revolver, bullet holes, an axe, a saw, a butcher's knife and a pair of bloodstained shoes that were thought to have belonged to John Dick. Four thousand dollars in cash and a large number of streetcar tickets were also found. This last find presumably represented the 'money and tickets belonging to the company' that the anonymous female had spoken about.

Evelyn, her father and Bill Bohozuk were then charged with what Canadians had come to call the 'Torso Murder'. The trial took place at the Hamilton Courthouse. On 16 October 1946 Evelyn was found guilty of murdering her husband. She was sentenced to death by hanging. However, her sentence was overturned after an appeal by her defence lawyer. It was ruled that the trial judge had improperly instructed the jury. Not only that, the police had erred by improperly admitting into evidence seven of Evelyn's contradictory statements. This notable victory was credited to J. J. Robinette, who was considered Canada's greatest trial lawyer. The famed Robinette went on to defend Evelyn in her second trial, which resulted in an acquittal.

Bill Bohozuk walked away from his trial a free man after Evelyn refused to testify – she was the sole witness. However, he had another trial to face. Bohozuk and Evelyn had both been charged with the murder of Peter David White. When Evelyn stood in court it was revealed that no one had seen the infant since she had taken it out of the hospital. In fact, she had arrived home without the child. She had told her mother that the Children's Aid Society had taken Peter for adoption – but this story was easily disproved in court. In the end, the jury found Evelyn guilty of manslaughter.

When it was Bohozuk's turn to stand trial, the very same evidence was presented. However, there was little to connect him to the infant's death. He had never lived in the house where Peter's body was found and the Red Cross uniform was certainly not his.

Once again the prosecution relied on Evelyn's testimony, but as before she refused to take the stand against her lover. Bohozuk maintained that he had not met Evelyn until after Peter was born. He also claimed that their friendship was never more than casual.

His testimony was supported by his wife, the jury was convinced and he was found not guilty.

The prosecution then made a second attempt at convicting Bohozuk for the murder of John Dick. But without Evelyn the prosecution had no case and predictably she refused to take the stand. The only person to be convicted for the murder of John Dick was Evelyn's father, Donald MacLean, who entered a plea bargain that saw him convicted as an accessory after the fact. He was sentenced to a five-year prison term.

Evelyn had been cleared of the murder of her husband but she still had to answer for the death of her baby. She was sentenced to life imprisonment. She spent 11 years in Kingston Penitentiary before being released on parole. After she had been given a new identity by a dedicated civil servant, she went back into the normal world and was never heard from again.

In 2001, author Brian Vallée brought to light a curious fact. Evelyn had been given a full pardon under Canada's rarely employed Royal Prerogative of Mercy provision. Without explanation, her record had been expunged and her files had been forever sealed. It seemed that Evelyn had also enjoyed a brief reunion with her daughter Heather at some point. But she would not even reveal her new identity to her only surviving child.

NANCY 'NANNIE' DOSS
'the Giggling Granny'

When she became famous – or infamous – 'Nannie', or Nancy, Doss was 47 years old. She was not an old woman by any means, yet in Eisenhower's America she became known as 'the Giggling Granny'. It was a misleading nickname, because it hid a past that included a good deal of drinking, fraud, sexual promiscuity and murder.

Nancy Hazle, later Doss, was born in Blue Mountain, Alabama on 4 November 1905. Her parents were farmers. She experienced a childhood that was anything but pleasant because her irritable father forced her to spend most of her out of school hours working on the farm. Not only that, the daily grind of chores was accompanied by poverty. The biggest thrill of her early life came at the age of seven, when she and her family boarded a train to visit a relative in another part of Alabama. However, this small vacation would be marred by an accident. When the train made an emergency stop Nannie was flung forward and hit her head on the iron bars of the seat in front. She claimed that she experienced blackouts for several months afterwards, followed by a lifetime of severe headaches. Later on, she would blame her murderous behaviour on this incident.

Nannie's contact with the opposite sex was limited to the classroom, because her father, James Hazle, did not want his daughters to get any romantic ideas. He feared that he would lose the bulk of his workforce if his daughters got married. So anything that might attract male attention was outlawed, including cosmetics, pleasing hairstyles and flattering dresses. He also forbade his daughters to attend any social gatherings.

Then in 1921, at the age of 15, Nannie went to work at the Linen Thread Company. No doubt her father thought the factory job would be good for the family, bringing in some badly needed money. However, it meant that James could no longer keep an eye on his daughter. She soon met a handsome local boy named Charley Braggs. When she brought him home to meet her parents, James must have realized that Nannie would one day get married. With such an attractive daughter matrimony was inevitable. In any case, Charley was a cut above most of the boys out there. For one thing, he doted on his mother, whom he supported through his work at the Linen Thread Company. That sort of filial devotion would certainly have appealed to James.

The couple were married four days after their first meeting. They moved in with Charley's mother. Nannie found her new mother-in-law a challenge right from the very beginning. She was a demanding woman who manipulated the couple by feigning ill-health. Young as she was, Nannie was forced to stay in at night in order to play cards with her mother-in-law at the kitchen table.

CLANDESTINE OUTINGS

Two years into the marriage, when she was just 17 years

old, Nannie gave birth to her first child, a daughter she named Melvina. By 1927, she was the mother of three more daughters. There was little chance of a social life for Nannie. She had to stay at home with her young children and her ageing mother-in-law. It is not surprising, then, that the young woman turned to drink. She began sneaking out to the local bars, where she enjoyed the attention of a variety of men. These clandestine outings were pretty easy to organize – Charley, the man who doted on his mother, had little time for his wife. He, too, was enjoying sexual dalliances with a number of partners. He would often disappear for days on end. However, these excursions were detrimental to his marriage and the family's finances.

In 1927, Nannie gave birth to her fourth child, Florine. Not long afterwards the two middle Bragg girls suddenly died. Seemingly healthy in the early morning, both were dead by noon. Though the deaths appeared suspicious the authorities took no action – but Charley suspected foul play. He left Nannie, taking Melvina with him. Months passed without any word from Charley, so when his mother died Nannie had no way of contacting him. Then suddenly, a little more than a year after he had disappeared, Charley came back. Melvina was with him, but so too was the woman with whom he had been living. Nannie was soon sent packing, together with Melvina and Florine. Her only option was to move back to her parents' house. She then took a job at a cotton mill. While Nannie's father might not have been very pleased with the situation, her mother enjoyed caring for her two granddaughters.

As always, Nannie enjoyed the attention she received from her male workmates. However, she set her sights higher when it came to matrimony. She began fishing for prospects by responding to personal advertisements that had been placed in the local newspaper. By this means she hooked a 23-year-old named Frank Harrelson. Like the men she came into contact with on a daily basis, he was a factory worker. What set him apart from the others was an element of sophistication – he wrote poetry – and his movie star good looks.

Nannie married Frank in 1929, after a brief courtship.

She then moved to Jacksonville, Frank's home town, with her daughters. This might have been the stormiest of her five marriages, but it was also the longest. For 16 years Nannie put up with physical abuse and her husband's alcoholism, while she was struggling to raise Melvina and Florine. It probably came as something of a relief when both girls got married at a young age – at least they were out of the house.

BECOMING A GRANDMOTHER

In 1943, at the age of 37, Nannie became a grandmother. Melvina had given birth to a son, Robert. Two years later, her eldest daughter went into labour for the second time. It was not an easy delivery, but Nannie sat at her bedside throughout the birth. She wiped her daughter's brow and provided words of encouragement. After enduring many hours of great pain, the expectant mother finally gave birth to a daughter.

Exhausted by the ordeal, Melvina's husband fell asleep in a chair close to the bed, while the new mother drifted in and out of consciousness. Their rest was broken when the baby girl died in Nannie's arms, less than an hour after her birth. The infant's death seemed such a mystery. Despite the difficult delivery, the newborn had appeared healthy and strong. That said, Melvina remembered having had some sort of vision while she had been in her semi-conscious state. Nannie had stuck a hatpin in the baby's head. Had it been a dream? A hallucination? Surely her mind had been playing tricks on her. Six months later, Melvina's son, Robert, also died under mysterious circumstances. He had been staying with Nannie at the time. Robert's death was recorded as asphyxia, though no one was ever able to determine the exact cause. A few months later, the grieving grandmother received $500 from a life insurance policy she had taken out on her grandson.

Only weeks later, in August 1945, Nannie's husband Frank also died. His final hours were spent in considerable pain, as one might expect – he had consumed a quantity of rat poison. Frank's widow was not a single woman for very long. It is quite possible that she married a man named Hendrix within a year of Frank's death. While the truth about Mr Hendrix remains unknown, Nannie certainly married Arlie Lanning, a labourer, in 1947.

For some reason Nannie appears to have been attracted to alcoholics and womanizers. Charley and Frank had both fitted this description and Arlie carried on with the tradition.

Needless to say, Nannie's latest marriage was no better than her previous failed attempts at wedded bliss. Leaving Arlie to drink himself into a stupor, Nannie would disappear from their Lexington, Kentucky home for weeks at a time, often visiting sickly relatives.

The caring, generous Nannie became a well-respected and well-liked figure. She joined the Lexington Methodist Church and became a dedicated member of its ladies' auxiliary. Parishioners had a great deal of sympathy for Nannie. The poor soul was married to a man who drank and slept around. No one would ever have suspected that this generous caring woman had once behaved in much the same way. Arlie died of suspected heart failure in February 1950. He had been bedridden during the last days of his life, when he had displayed mysterious flu-like symptoms.

Two months later, tragedy again befell the 44-year-old widow. The house in which she and her late husband had spent their wedded lives had burned down. If there was any luck to be found it lay in the fact that Nannie had left the house just moments before the fire, taking her expensive television set with her.

According to Arlie's will, the house should have been inherited by his sister. However, Arlie's final wish did not prevent Nannie from cashing the insurance cheque for herself.

Bad fortune appeared to follow Nannie right through the first half of 1950. Now homeless, she moved in with Arlie's mother, but the old woman soon died. After that, she left Lexington behind for the small Alabama city of Gadsden, where she dedicated herself to the care of her ailing sister, Dovie. Despite Nannie's care, though, the bedridden woman was dead by the end of June.

On the hunt for a new husband, Nannie turned to a new source, the Diamond Circle Club, a company catering to the lovelorn, After paying her $15 annual fee, the middle-aged widow started to receive monthly newsletters containing lists of prospective spouses. She settled on Richard L. Morton, a retired businessman from Emporia, Kansas. Tall, dark, handsome, and more than willing to flash the cash, Richard looked like the perfect partner. In October 1952 Nannie and Richard were married. Nannie realized the truth about her latest man just weeks after the wedding ring had been slipped on to her finger. Despite his displays of extravagance, Richard had no money. In fact, he was in debt to very nearly everyone he knew – everyone but a mistress who lived in the very same small Kansas city.

Two months into her marriage to Richard, Nannie was again going through the personal advertisements. She told her correspondents that she was a widow, a description that was a little premature. Nannie had already begun making plans to rid herself of Richard when news of her father's death arrived from Blue Mountain. Her widowed mother Louisa then left Alabama for Kansas. She had come to stay with her daughter and son-in-law, but her visit was destined to be a short one. Within 48 hours she was dead.

Three months later, Richard joined his mother-in-law in death.

HUSBAND NO. 5

True to form, Nannie was not without a husband for long. In fact, she set a new personal speed record with her next spouse. Sam Doss proposed just weeks after she had buried Richard. Sam was a state highway inspector in Tulsa, Oklahoma. Honest and reliable, he had been among those corresponding with the 'widowed' Nannie during Richard's final months. He was like no other man Nannie had ever met. Not a drop of liquor touched his lips, he did not chase women and he would not think of raising a fist to his wife. Sam proved to be handy around the house and he enjoyed helping his new wife prepare the meals.

Just the man Nannie had been looking for, it seems. But the relationship was far from idyllic in her eyes. True, Sam had a good deal of money, but his wealth had been amassed through decades of frugal living. He even frowned on the gossip magazines and romance novels that Nannie devoured. They were a waste of time and cash, he thought. Eventually, Nannie rebelled. She moved back to Alabama, leaving her husband behind. Sam pursued her with letters. He pleaded for forgiveness and promised her a more luxurious lifestyle. The highway inspector even went so far as to transfer his savings into a joint account. Finally, he made certain that Nannie would continue living in comfort even after his death – he took out two life insurance policies.

All this dramatic activity – the proposal, the wedding, the separation, the reconciliation, the financial arrangements and the life insurance policies – took place over the course of just three months. In September, Sam became violently ill after having eaten a tasty slice of his wife's prune cake. The ailing man took to his bed and was later taken by his doctor to the local hospital. There he stayed for 23 days, while he was treated for what had been diagnosed as a severe infection of the digestive tract. It was not until 5 October that he was finally well enough to return home. That evening, Nannie served Richard a roast pork dinner accompanied by a fresh cup of coffee.

He was dead before the following day had dawned.

None of Nannie's previous murders had attracted any suspicion of foul play. However, with Sam's death her luck had finally run out. The doctor who had cared for her husband during his hospital stay had been shocked to learn of his sudden death. An autopsy was ordered, which established that Sam had not died of a digestive tract infection. The cause of death had been a massive dose of arsenic.

When she was taken into custody, Nannie denied any knowledge of the arsenic. She spent her time reading cheap romantic fiction, such as Romantic Heart magazine, while investigators slowly began uncovering the trail of death she had left in her wake. When she was confronted with each new finding, Nannie just giggled. It was only when they took away her reading material that she finally confessed to Sam's murder.

'He wouldn't let me watch my favourite programmes on the television,' she complained, 'and he made me sleep without the fan on the hottest nights. He was a miser and... well, what's a woman to do under those conditions?'

Nannie struck a deal with the police, in which she would tell them about her past husbands in exchange for the return of her magazine. All of her husbands had been 'dullards', she said. 'If their ghosts are in this room they're either drunk or sleeping.'

The bodies of Frank, Arlie and Richard were exhumed, together with those of her mother, her sister and her nephew. And then there was Arlie's mother. They had all died of arsenic poisoning or asphyxia. Despite the findings, Nannie was charged with the only murder that had taken place in Oklahoma – that of her last husband, Sam Doss. On 17 May 1955 she had no alternative but to plead guilty. The court sentenced her to life imprisonment. She escaped the electric chair only because of her sex.

Nannie became something of a celebrity when she was finally placed behind bars. Several leading publications, including *Life* magazine, sent along journalists to interview her. Charley Braggs, her first husband, also became a media star, but this time for the right reasons. As the only husband to survive marriage to Nannie he had a fascinating story to tell. He spoke quite openly about the troubled nature of their relationship, including the adultery. 'To tell you the truth, I was glad when she was off. It got to a point I was afraid to eat anything she cooked.'

'The Giggling Granny' died of leukaemia on 2 June 1965, several months short of what would have been her 60th birthday.

KATHLEEN FOLBIGG
Her father's
daughter

Kathleen Megan Folbigg has the doubtful distinction of being Australia's first convicted female serial killer. She is imprisoned at Silverwater Woman's Correctional Centre, 9 miles (15 kilometres) from downtown Sydney.

Born in Sydney on 14 June 1967, Kathleen was placed in a church orphanage before her second birthday. At the age of three, she was adopted by the Marlboroughs, a loving foster family in suburban Newcastle. Kathleen – or Kathy, as she preferred to be called – was not the best student. She left school before her sixteenth birthday in order to take the first in a series of low-wage, low-skilled jobs. Within six years, she had met and married her husband, Craig Folbigg, a steel worker. The newlyweds set up home in the Newcastle suburb of Mayfield.

Kathy was pregnant by the time the couple's first anniversary came along. She gave birth to a baby boy named Caleb on the first day of February 1989. The young mother had experienced a good full term pregnancy, which had resulted in the birth of a seemingly healthy child. Yet four days after Caleb was born the new mother and her child were back at the hospital. Kathy told doctors that while she had been feeding the newborn baby she had noticed that he had been having some trouble breathing. Caleb was diagnosed as having a 'lazy larynx', which was not seen as a serious condition.

TRAGEDY STRIKES

Fourteen days passed without incident. Then shortly before three o'clock on the morning of 19 February Craig was awoken by Kathy's screams. They were coming from the baby's room. His wife was standing at the side of the crib. She was weeping over Caleb's lifeless body. The cause of death, after just 18 days of life, was listed as SIDS – Sudden Infant Death Syndrome.

By September, seven months after Caleb's death, Kathy was again pregnant. On 3 June 1990, she gave birth to Patrick, another baby boy. At that stage, there was nothing to suggest that Patrick was not completely healthy. However, shortly after three o'clock on the morning of 19 October 1990, Craig was again jolted out of slumber by his wife's screams. Running to the baby's room, he saw Kathy standing over the cot. Patrick was not breathing. The steel worker picked the baby up and began resuscitation. Though the baby survived, no one was able to determine the cause of the medical emergency. During the myriad tests that followed, the baby was discovered to be epileptic and blind. Clearly, Patrick had not been as healthy as the doctors had originally believed.

On 13 February 1991, just days before the second anniversary of Caleb's death, Craig was at work when he received a frantic phone call from Kathy. 'It's happened again,' she said. He reached home just as the ambulance arrived. This time the father could do nothing to save his son. At eight months of age, Patrick was dead. After an autopsy had been conducted, the cause of the child's death was recorded as an epileptic fit, which had resulted in an 'acute asphyxiating event'.

Following this sad affair the couple moved to Thornton, a suburb of Maitland, which lay approximately 99 miles (160 kilometres) to the north of Sydney. It was there, on 14 October 1992, that the third Folbigg child was born. This time, Kathy gave birth to a baby girl, who was named Sarah Kathleen. But disaster struck again. In the early hours of 30 August 1993, the ten-month-old infant stopped breathing. According to Kathy, baby Sarah had caught some sort of cold and was having trouble sleeping.

After losing their daughter, the Folbiggs moved yet again. This time they settled in Singleton, a town on the Hunter River, about an hour's drive from Newcastle. In the space of only four and a half years the couple had endured the deaths of three children. It was two years before Kathy became pregnant again. Then on 7 August 1997 she gave birth to Laura, another baby girl. At first Laura appeared to be quite healthy, just like the Folbigg children that had come before her. In view of the past tragedies, however, her sleep patterns and her breathing were monitored very closely throughout August and into September. Unlike her dead siblings, Laura managed to celebrate her first birthday. In fact, she lived nearly 19 months before developing what her mother described as a cold. Then at about noon on 1 March 1999, Kathy called for an ambulance. The attendants arrived to find the mother 'performing CPR on her daughter on the breakfast bar'. It was all in vain – Laura was dead. This time, however, Laura's death could not be written off to SIDS: she was simply too old. After performing an autopsy, the coroner ordered a police investigation.

Meanwhile, the strain on the Folbigg marriage had taken its toll. Kathy left her husband, taking very few possessions with her. Much of what she left behind was personal in nature, nothing more so than the diaries that Craig found while he was cleaning the house. Reading their contents, the abandoned husband said that he wanted to vomit. The diaries contained the thoughts of a tormented woman, who had often been jealous of the attention her babies were receiving. Kathy recorded 'flashes of rage, resentment and hatred' towards her children. Concerning Laura, she wrote:

> *I feel like the worst mother on this earth. Scared that she will leave me now. Like Sarah did. I knew I was short-tempered and cruel sometimes to her and she left. With a bit of help. She's a fairly good-natured baby – thank goodness, it has saved her from the fate of her siblings. I'm sure she's met everyone and they've told her, don't be a bad or sickly kid, mum may, you know, crack. They've warned her – good.*

Kathy's diaries were handed over to Bernard Ryan, the detective assigned to the case. They would ultimately be used as evidence against her in a court of law.

It took two years to put the case together. Tests determined that none of the four Folbigg children had suffered any genetic or viral disorders. Further investigation revealed that all of the deaths were inconsistent with SIDS – each child had been lying face upwards and all of them had been still warm when the ambulance attendants had arrived. During the course of the investigation, Ryan uncovered a very disturbing story from Kathy's past. In December 1968, a couple of weeks before Christmas, Kathy's father had killed her mother. She was stabbed 24 times outside her home in suburban Sydney. After his murderous act, Kathy's father reportedly knelt down beside the body. He kissed his dead lover and whispered, 'I'm sorry, darling. I had to do it'. According to a witness he then said, 'I had to kill her because she'd kill my child'. The child in question was Kathy.

It is not so surprising that Kathy knew nothing of the tragedy until her late teens. Her birth parents were poles apart from the caring couple that had adopted her. Kathy's birth father was a petty thief with ties to organized crime, while her birth mother was addicted to gambling and alcohol. The uncovering of the tragedy that had taken place between Kathy's parents made one particular passage in the diary stand out: 'Obviously, I am my father's daughter'.

JUSTICE SERVED

On 19 April 2001 Kathy was arrested and charged with the murders of all four of her children. When her foster mother learned of the arrest, she sent Kathy all of her childhood photographs, accompanied by a letter. 'Kathleen Megan, I WILL NEVER FORGIVE YOU,' she wrote. The prosecution presented the medical evidence that had been amassed over the previous two years, adding that the diaries were a 'partial admission of guilt'. Witnesses, including Kathy's foster sister, Lea Brown, supported the self-portrait that Kathy had penned. It was noted, for example, that Kathy had expressed no real grief at the funerals of her four children. The court was also presented with a video tape that showed a seemingly healthy Laura swimming in her pool on the afternoon before her death.

In spite of all of the evidence to the contrary, the defence argued that all four Folbigg children had been sickly. They called a forensic pathologist named Roger Byard as a witness, but even he was forced to admit that it was possible that each of the children had died from deliberate suffocation. On 21 May 2003, Kathleen Folbigg was found guilty on three counts of murder, one count of manslaughter and one count of maliciously inflicting grievous bodily harm. She was sentenced to 40 years imprisonment, with the possibility of parole after 30 years. On appeal, her sentence was reduced to a prison sentence of 30 years, with a non-parole period of 25 years.

Craig Folbigg obtained a divorce and has since remarried. He was offered more than 200,000 Australian dollars for his story, but he turned it down, explaining that he just wanted to get on with his life.

TRACEY FRAME
the curvaceous
killer

Tracey Frame did not look anything like most people's idea of an accountant. The tall and curvaceous Texan was the sort of woman who would turn heads wherever she went.

In 1998, the 29-year-old bikini-clad Tracey was turning heads at Grapevine Lake, a playground for the affluent near Dallas, when she met David Nixon, a handsome 36-year-old real estate agent.

David had been immensely successful in business, but he had not experienced the same good fortune when it came to relationships. His second wife had left him only a month before he met Tracey. Though he was just beginning the process of another divorce, the real estate agent displayed no hesitation in pursuing a new relationship. It was, according to one friend, 'a real rebound thing'.

Tracey quickly took her place in the centre of David's life. The attractive brunette had her new boyfriend nearly all to herself. Nicholas, David's son by his first wife, Donna Lella, was the only other person in his life. David proved to be a very generous boyfriend. First of all, he bought Tracey a black version of his own white Lexus. Then before long she moved into his house in Grapevine, an affluent suburb of Dallas. They lived extremely well at that point. Nothing hindered their enjoyment of the finer things of life, such as good food, expensive cars and cruises.

They were still in the early stages of their relationship when the fighting began. Their arguments, many of which were witnessed by friends, were often about money. Tracey claimed that David was living far beyond his means. What is more, he was burdened by a gambling problem. According to Tracey, the fights would turn into shoving matches behind closed doors. She said that David would have been consumed by debt if it had not been for her. Things had reached such a point by the spring of

2002 that she had suggested that they part. However, in April she did something rather odd for a woman who had decided to leave. David arrived home one evening to find that Tracey had changed all of the locks in his house. He had to call the police to gain entry.

WITHOUT A TRACE

Ten days later, Nicholas tried to reach his father by telephone. Even though the boy left a message, the call was never returned. When two more days passed without any word from David, Nicholas's mother filed a missing person report with the Grapevine Police Department. In doing so, Donna Lella pointed a finger directly at Tracey. She was certain that Tracey had something to do with the disappearance.

Donna's report, filed just before midnight, became the first in a fast-moving series of dramatic events. A little more than two hours later, in the early hours of 22 April, the mystery of David's whereabouts was solved. A motorist driving through an industrial park in Grand Prairie, roughly 18 miles (30 kilometres) south of Grapevine, came across a storm drain with flames shooting from it. He sought help from a security guard, an off-duty police officer, who managed to put the blaze out with a fire extinguisher.

It was then that the two men saw what had been burning – it was a human body, wrapped in a tarpaulin and an electric blanket. The remains had been so consumed by the fire that immediate identification was not possible. However, the police were as sure as they could be that the missing man had been found. Several hours later, Tracey was interviewed at the Grapevine house. She told investigators that she had not seen David since Thursday, the day before Nicholas made his unreturned phone call.

While the police were canvassing the neighbourhood, they heard from a man named Darby Taylor. He had not seen David for several days, but he reported that something unusual had taken place on the previous Sunday. A rental truck had appeared in David's driveway. It had been backed right up to the garage. The next day, it was gone. For what purpose, police wondered, had the truck been rented? By the afternoon, roughly 12 hours after its discovery, Grapevine police confirmed that the burning body had indeed been David's. But the real estate agent had not died as a result of the fire. His death had been caused by a gunshot wound that had passed straight through his body, destroying his lungs and his heart in the process. When Tracey was told that David's body had been found, police found her reaction rather curious. 'How did they identify him?' she asked.

POLICE QUESTIONING

Tracey was taken into the police station for questioning. When she was asked about the truck that had been seen in the driveway, she told investigators that she had rented the vehicle on the Friday, but had only kept it overnight. A cursory check into her claim revealed that the truck had indeed been rented on the Friday – together with a furniture trolley – but it could not have been returned until shortly after 9.00pm on Sunday at the very earliest. The clerk who had dealt with the paperwork recalled that Tracey had left a white Lexus behind when she had driven the truck away.

The mystery surrounding the current location of David's white Lexus was soon solved. That evening, the manager of a supermarket near David's house reported that a white Lexus had been sitting in his car park since Sunday evening. The seemingly abandoned car was, of course, David Nixon's. The security cameras at the supermarket had not only recorded the arrival of David's white Lexus – there was also a rental truck, and what appeared to be Tracey's black Lexus, on the video recording. The rental truck was seen arriving on Saturday afternoon, while the black Lexus turned up on Sunday night. A woman who looked like Tracey got out of her car, shopped at the supermarket and then drove away in the rental truck. She returned at 1.34am on the following Monday, about half an hour before her boyfriend's body was discovered. This time she was driving David's white Lexus.

On Wednesday, 24 April, Tracey was arrested and charged with David's death.

During Tracey's trial, her defence team argued that she was not the only person who stood to benefit by David's death. They suggested that his first wife Donna also had something to gain. It was noted that Nicholas was the beneficiary in a life insurance policy that his father had recently taken out. Perhaps that was why Donna had been the first to suggest that Tracey was responsible for the realtor's disappearance. The prosecution countered by telling the court that Donna's actions had been motivated by nothing more than the fact that her son was upset when he was not able to contact his father.

Now 13 years of age, Nicholas took the stand. He testified that his father had once shown him a gun that he had kept in his safe. However, the firearm was now nowhere to be found. The prosecution alleged that Tracey had used the gun to kill David and had then disposed of it at some point over the weekend in question. Then the car park surveillance video was produced, along with the store's records, which revealed that Tracey's store discount card had been used to make a saving of 19 cents. However, the accused denied that the woman on the footage was her. She claimed that she had been visiting her parents in Arlington at the time, which was 16 miles (25 kilometres) away. What she could not explain was the use of her store discount card. 'So, I don't have an answer for it,' she told one reporter, 'but I don't think that I would use a discount card if I was trying to sneak around town.'

It was also apparent that David's mobile telephone had been used after his disappearance. A call had been made to H & H Janitorial Supply. Not only that, Tracey had gone into the store on the day after David's disappearance. She was looking for a way of removing bloodstains. The store had recommended muriatic acid, which they did not carry. However, the supermarket that Tracey visited hours before David's body was found did sell the product. The security video clearly showed her buying muriatic acid and other items. These same purchases were later found in David's house.

On 9 March 2005, the day that would have been David's 43rd birthday, Tracey was found guilty. She was later sentenced to 40 years' imprisonment. Tracey will be eligible for parole in 2024.

RITA GLUZMAN
the Refusenik
murderer

Yakov Gluzman would not have been considered **a famous man**, yet his name had featured in news stories at various points in his life. In the late 1960s, for example, he and his wife Rita had garnered international attention as Refuseniks. That is, they were Soviet Jews who were neither allowed to practise their faith nor emigrate. Then in 1971 the Russians permitted Rita to leave the Soviet Union. She used the opportunity to mount a high profile campaign on behalf of the Refuseniks, particularly Yakov. Her efforts bore fruit because in 1972 Rita and Yakov were reunited in Israel, where they lived for five years before moving to the United States. Meanwhile Yakov's work in cancer research had brought him another kind of media attention, as well as great wealth. In 1996, Yakov made the headlines yet again when he was hacked into pieces and thrown into New Jersey's Passaic River.

Rita and Yakov's early years in the United States are thought to have been happy ones. Yakov, a microbiologist, found work at Cold Spring Harbor, New York. He was part of a research team led by the Nobel Prize winner James D. Watson who, together with Francis Crick, had discovered the molecular structure of DNA. During his time at Cold Spring Harbor, Yakov developed a technique that was soon adopted by cancer researchers the world over. While the accomplishment might not have made headlines, it made him famous within the scientific community. The couple adapted well to their new life in the United States and they seemed content to raise their son, Illan, as an American.

THE AMERICAN DREAM

Yakov and Rita followed the American dream together. When Lederle Laboratories of Rockland County, New York offered the émigré a job that carried a salary of $180,000 a year, he leapt at the opportunity. The young family left Cold Spring Harbor and bought a massive house in the affluent borough of Upper Saddle River, New Jersey. Riches came their way at a rapid pace. Yakov then funded a small electronics company, ECI Technology, that Rita was going to head. But Rita had caught the capitalist spending bug. She spent thousands of dollars each month on furs, clothes, cosmetics, personal trainers, salons and the grooming of her dog. Rita then came to resent her husband's more modest lifestyle. To her, the house that had once seemed so impressive became a 'shack'. Yakov was earning more than ever, yet he refused to increase his spending to match.

Another area of contention involved ECI Technology. Rita had been placed in charge of the company, but its fortunes had declined as a result. By the end of 1994, it appeared that the once famous Refusenik couple were through. Yakov told select friends that he was in love with another woman, Raisa Korenblit, and was seriously thinking of moving to Israel to be with her. Although the microbiologist had told Rita that he wanted a divorce, they remained together in their Rockland County home for another month. Then, in January 1995, Yakov moved into a two-room apartment in New York State, not far from his work. He left his wife with $90,000 to cover her day-to-day expenses, but this proved no match for the extravagant lifestyle she had adopted.

In January of 1996, one month after Yakov had filed for divorce, Rita was arrested after attempting to steal some insignificant items from a New Jersey pharmacy. For Rita, life was in a death spiral. She needed a way to regain control – and so she came up with a sinister plan. Her cousin Vladimir Zelenin would help her. Vladimir was a 40-year-old Russian émigré who had arrived in the United States 11 months earlier. To Rita, he must have seemed the perfect accomplice. After all, Vladimir had something less than a snow-white background. In Russia, he had often found himself on the wrong side of the law. And then there was the matter of his wife's murder, which was why Vladimir had left the country of his birth. He had lied to immigration authorities by claiming that he had been made a widower as the result of an anti-Semitic attack.

What was more, Vladimir was one of Rita's employees and it was thanks to her efforts that he had entered the United States. Rita convinced her cousin that a divorce would mean the end of the company. He would lose his job, his car and his home, she said, and he would have to return to Russia.

For the next few weeks, Rita tried her best to win her estranged husband's goodwill. With this new attitude, she was able to get a copy of the key to Yakov's apartment. Then, she waited... but not for long. Rita amassed a bag of tools – a hacksaw, an axe, some knives and a scalpel – and on the evening of 6 April 1994 she and Vladimir drove to Yakov's apartment and let themselves in. They both knew that the 48-year-old microbiologist spent his Saturday evenings at the laboratory.

STRIKING THE ATTACK

At approximately 11.30pm Yakov entered his darkened apartment. Vladimir struck the first blow and Yakov fell to the floor. And then Rita started in with her axe. She swung with such abandon that Vladimir was hit, too.

He suffered a bad cut to his hand. Ignoring her injured cousin's pain, Rita took a knife and plunged it into Yakov's chest.

The two murderers then dragged the corpse into the bathroom, where they began chopping and cutting. They removed Yakov's fingertips, nose and lips, in order to prevent the body from being identified. The work took much of the night. At one point, Rita turned her attention to the small apartment. She scrubbed it clean while Vladimir continued dismembering her husband.

When the work was done, the remains of Yakov Gluzman's body lay in 66 pieces, which had been stuffed into ten black plastic garbage bags. Another bag contained their bloody instruments. All of the bags were then distributed between the two waiting cars – Yakov's Nissan Maxima and a Ford Taurus belonging to ECI Technology. The two murderers planned to drive both cars to ECI's offices, some 30 or so miles (50 kilometres) away. Vladimir was then going to drive Rita home before returning to ECI.

The Passaic River ran behind the building so he could

easily throw the garbage bags into the moving water without going too far from Rita's premises. Having disposed of the body, he would then return the car to the parking lot of Yakov's apartment building. All would take place under cover of night.

BEHIND SCHEDULE

The problem was that Rita and Vladimir were running well behind schedule. Neither of them had dismembered a body before, so the process had taken much longer than they had intended. But there would be further delays. While loading the black plastic bags, Vladimir had set off the Nissan Maxima's alarm. Anxious not to be seen, Rita insisted that they get into the Taurus and drive away. Some time passed before they dared return to the apartment parking lot. Then there was the problem of Vladimir's hand, which required a visit to a pharmacy, where Rita spent $32.02 on bandages.

By the time Vladimir dropped Rita off at her home the sun was high in the sky. Even though he was well behind schedule, Vladimir made his way back to ECI as planned.

The driving was easy because the roads were relatively free of cars. It was Easter Sunday. Vladimir parked at the back of the office building and opened both car boots so that he could begin disposing of Yakov's remains. Just as he began, he was spotted by the driver of a police cruiser that was moving through the area. The police officer, named Richard Freeman, watched as Vladimir took a bag from the boot of one of the cars, before walking to the shore and tossing it into the river. When Freeman moved to confront the émigré, he had assumed that he was about to issue a ticket for illegal dumping. However, as the police officer drew closer, he saw real fear in Vladimir's eyes. The officer then noticed the bloodstains on the man's trousers and shoes. Not only that, the 40-year-old was wearing a surgical glove, which was also covered in blood.

Vladimir was taken into custody. Questioning proved difficult at first, owing to the fact that he spoke precious little English. It was some time before the police managed to get a Russian interpreter, a delay that worked in Rita's favour. When her cousin failed to show up, the now widowed Mrs Gluzman knew that her already shaky plan had fallen completely apart. She quickly left her home and drove into New York State, stopping along the way to steal the licence plates from a parked car. Her ultimate destination was an odd choice. She was making for Cold Spring Harbor, the community in which she had begun her pursuit of the American Dream. When she got there she managed to break into a small bungalow. There she rested, contemplating her next move.

Her mistake was that she overstayed her welcome. On 12 April, six days after the murder, a cleaning lady entered Rita's hideout. The murderer managed to flee by climbing out of a window, but she left her passport behind in the process. Then she made her way to Blackford Hall, part of the Cold Spring Harbor Laboratory in which her deceased husband had once worked, and tried to blend in with the crowd. But some security guards were looking for the woman who had broken into the bungalow, so she was picked up almost immediately. It is entirely possible that she would have been charged with trespassing, or at worst burglary, had it not been for the fact that the head of security recognized Rita from the time the Gluzmans had lived in Cold Spring Harbor. He knew that Yakov Gluzman had been killed... and he knew that the police were looking for his widow.

By this time, Vladimir had been charged with second degree murder, for which he would eventually receive a sentence amounting to 22 and a half years in prison. The problem facing the prosecutors was that under New York State law a murder case cannot be based on the testimony of an accomplice alone. There either had to be a witness to Rita's part in the murder or the authorities had to present some very compelling evidence. It seemed an impossible challenge. Rita's fingerprints were present at the scene of the murder, but they would be there anyway – the couple had experienced occasional thaws in their acrimonious relationship. There was also a video recording of Rita's purchase of bandages for Vladimir. But that would only make her an accessory after the fact, at best.

LEGAL LOOPHOLE

The solution to the problem was both unprecedented and daring – Rita was charged under the 1994 Domestic

Violence Statute. This law allowed for the prosecution of a person who had crossed state lines in order to commit an act of domestic violence. In this case the border was between New Jersey and New York. Vladimir's testimony would then be admissible and Rita would make history as the first woman ever to be charged under the statute. Although Rita denied any involvement in her husband's murder, the jury believed Vladimir. The accused had done herself no favours by her aggressive behaviour in the courtroom.

On 30 April 1997, just before Rita was sentenced, a letter from Yakov Gluzman's parents was read in court.

'For 25 years she gradually demolished him emotionally and in the 26th year she dismembered him physically. By her evil act Rita has ruined the life of her son, whom she left fatherless, and marked him with the stigma of a mother convicted for murder.'

Judge Barrington D. Parker handed down a life sentence with no possibility of parole.

MARIE HILLEY
the three lives of
a poisoner

Blue Mountain, Alabama, does not exist any more. In 2003 the insignificant little mill town was absorbed into the neighbouring city of Anniston. Some say it barely existed in the first place. Its population had never risen above a thousand or two. However, in 1953 it suddenly found itself in the spotlight. It was the birthplace and hometown of Nannie Doss, one of the country's most notorious and active serial killers. Three decades later, the people of Blue Mountain would learn that their tiny community had spawned another female serial killer.

Audrey Marie Frazier was born on 4 June 1933, 18 years after Nannie Doss. Her parents, Huey and Lucille Frazier, worked in the local mills, like nearly everyone in

Blue Mountain. In fact, Marie's mother was employed by the Linen Thread Company, where Nannie Doss had once worked. Because Marie was an only child, she was in a better situation than many of her playmates. Whereas most of them came from large families of limited means, Marie's parents were able to do a little bit more for her.

Very early in life, Marie had decided that she would rise above the bleak life that her parents lived. She was determined to complete high school, a rare accomplishment in Blue Mountain, and then become a secretary. In 1945, the year that she reached the age of 12, the family moved 2 miles (3 kilometres) down the road to Anniston. The move was a significant one for Marie. She would now attend Quintard Junior High School.

Whereas her old classmates had been the children of mill workers, she now attended classes with the sons and daughters of the mill owners. She adapted well to her new surroundings – her grades were high and she joined the student council. At the end of her first year, she was named 'Prettiest Girl at Quintard' in the high school yearbook.

When she left Quintard to go on to Anniston High School, it seemed obvious that the academically-gifted Marie would complete her secondary school education. Still intending to become a secretary, she joined the Commercial Club, an organization for those planning careers in the field. As she progressed from grade to grade, always achieving good marks, it seemed that other possibilities were opening up – she became a member of the Future Teachers of America.

TURNING HEADS

By the time she entered her final years at Anniston High School, the 'Prettiest Girl' had become a beautiful young woman. Marie attracted a great deal of polite male attention in the school hallways, though her eyes fell on just one boy. His name was Frank Hilley and he was the son of a factory worker. He did not come from one of the mill-owning families. Even so, Frank tried his best to treat Marie as well as his circumstances would allow. He gave her gifts – whatever he could afford – and treated her to evenings out on the town.

Frank was a year older than his girlfriend, so he graduated from high school first. He then joined the Navy and was sent off to Guam. In May 1951 Frank took advantage of his first leave and married Marie. Because she was in her final months of high school, she stayed behind while her new husband crossed the country to his new assignment in Long Beach, California. Frank sent his pay cheques home to Marie, but he was unaware that she was spending all of the money. As a result, the couple had no funds when the time came for her to join him on the West Coast. It fell to Marie's new in-laws to pay for her trip.

Marie's extravagance continued in California, which led to the first serious rows of their marriage. Then in 1952 the couple moved to Boston, where Frank completed his tour of duty and was discharged. Marie was in the early weeks of pregnancy when she and her husband returned to Anniston. Fortunately, the couple were able to make a down payment on a modest house. Frank found work with Standard Foundry, while Marie got a job as a secretary – just as she had always intended.

On 11 November 1952, the couple's first child, Michael, or Mike, was born. Their second baby, Carol, would not arrive until 1960. The Hilleys did reasonably well in the intervening years. Frank was now foreman of the shipping department, while Marie had become an executive secretary. Though Frank had achieved a degree of stability in his employment, the same could not be said for his wife. Marie moved from job to job and company to company. Although her employers appreciated her qualities, she did not get on well with her colleagues. Marie combined a snobbish attitude with a twisted approach to office politics, which made her unpopular with her colleagues.

Nevertheless, she never seemed to want for work. No sooner had she left one job than another fell into her lap. But a foreman and a secretary could never earn enough to satisfy Marie's craving for the finer things in life. The couple lived within their means, but only just. However, while the Hilley children never wanted for material possessions, their father was the only one who paid them any attention. The feminine and proper Marie turned her back on the tomboyish Carol. When Frank tried to make up for his wife's coldness by developing a loving relationship with his daughter, Marie became jealous.

By 1971, Marie and Frank had reached their platinum wedding anniversary – but the marriage was in a very unhealthy state. The bride of 20 years had taken to taunting her husband by telling him that she was receiving love letters from a number of men in Anniston. Marie had also been slowly bringing the family to the point of bankruptcy. She had even rented a post office box so that she could receive bills without her husband's knowledge. And then she began falling behind with payments. Unknown to Frank, who had a reputation for always meeting his obligations on time, she had taken out several loans. It was only when his wife began to default that Frank became aware of the situation. This revelation, which came to light in the autumn of 1974, was soon matched by another one. Shortly afterwards, Frank arrived home early one day to find his wife in bed with her employer.

MYSTERY AFFLICTION

The reason Frank left Standard Foundry early that day

was that he had been feeling ill. Throughout the remainder of 1974 and into the new year, the shipping foreman's condition continued to deteriorate. Though he was prescribed all sorts of medications, Frank continued to vomit frequently and he experienced long periods of nausea. In the early hours of 23 May, he was found wandering about outside the house. He was taken to the hospital, where he was diagnosed with infectious hepatitis. In spite of being given a range of prescription drugs, his condition only deteriorated. Marie stayed by her husband's bedside. She was joined by Mike, their son, who was now a pastor. He was concerned that his father's hallucinations might cause him to leap out of the window.

In the early hours of 25 May, Mike left to collect his grandmothers, who wanted to visit Frank. By the time he returned his father was dead. Marie had not witnessed Frank's final moments – she had apparently been asleep at the time. Because the cause of death was recorded as infectious hepatitis, Marie received $31,000 from her husband's insurance policies. It did not make her wealthy, but it funded a spending spree. She bought herself a car, a quantity of jewellery and some fine clothes. Others benefited too. Her mother was given a diamond ring and the children received cars, appliances and furniture.

Frank's death appeared to have set off a series of unfortunate, often mysterious events. Marie claimed that small items were being stolen from her home. After her mother was diagnosed with cancer, the old woman moved into the Hilley home. Marie convinced her son and daughter-in-law, Mike and Teri, to move in as well. But then Teri became very ill after experiencing severe bouts of stomach pain. She was hospitalized on four different occasions and she suffered a miscarriage.

Eventually, Mike and Teri decided to move out. However, a fire broke out at the Hilley house on the evening before they were due to take possession of their new apartment. While repairs were made, Mike and Teri were forced to share their apartment with Marie, Lucille and Carol. Weeks later, just as the three women were preparing to leave, a fire broke out in the neighbouring flat. So Mike and Teri were obliged to move back into the Hilley house with Marie, Lucille and Carol. Other fires followed. Shortly after her mother succumbed to cancer, Marie reported that someone had started a fire in one of her closets. Another closet fire was later reported by Marie's neighbour, Doris Ford. Marie told the police that she had been receiving calls of a threatening nature. Doris reported the same experience.

When Mike and Teri moved to Pompano Beach, Florida, Marie thought it best to leave Anniston. She moved into her son and daughter-in-law's new home, but the arrangement only lasted a few months. After running up $600 on Mike's credit card, Marie returned to Anniston. Strangely enough, the peculiar chain of events began again. There were severed telephone lines and still more fires. In the midst of all of this, Marie began a long-distance relationship with Calvin Robertson, an old high school classmate who was now living in San Francisco. When he was informed that she had cancer, he sent money for treatment, which Marie promptly spent on expensive clothes. Eventually, the relationship came to an end when Robertson realized that he did not want to leave his wife.

In April of 1979, Marie's daughter Carol and her mother-in-law Carol (Carrie) Hilley were both attacked by bouts of nausea and vomiting. In the months that passed, Marie demonstrated a level of affection and solicitude that had been lacking during her daughter's childhood. The secretary became a regular visitor to her daughter's apartment. She cooked for her and she administered the medicines that had been prescribed for her mystery illness. Carol's health continued on its downward spiral until August. At that point, Marie was advised to take the young woman to a psychiatrist. When she did so, she informed the doctor that her daughter had been suicidal. After hearing that, he thought it best that Carol should be placed in the Carraway Methodist Hospital in Birmingham, where she was admitted to the psychiatric ward.

It was while her daughter was under observation that Marie was arrested for the first time. The charge had nothing to do with murder, attempted murder or arson. Marie had been writing bad cheques. Without Frank's salary, and with the money from his life insurance long gone, Marie had resorted to fraud to buy the material possessions she so desired.

Although she was released on bail, it started to become clear that life as she had known it was coming to an end. Mike had discovered that Marie had administered injections of some unknown substance to both his father and his sister. As a result, the pastor asked that his mother be kept away from Carol. Confronted with this request, Marie removed her daughter from the Carraway Hospital and took her to the University of Alabama Hospital in Birmingham. On 20 September, Marie was again arrested for bouncing cheques. This time, though, there was no bail. She was still in prison when toxicology reports indicated that Carol had for some time been suffering from arsenic poisoning.

Six days after her arrest on the cheque charges, Marie admitted that she had given injections to her mother and her daughter. However, she claimed that the substance had been medicine supplied to her by the mother of a nurse. In October, Frank's body was exhumed. Tests revealed the presence of arsenic. The police then discovered a bottle of the poison at an address in Anniston. Marie had lived there for a while when she returned from Florida. Then a pill bottle containing arsenic was found in Marie's handbag after she was arrested. Finally, Lucille's body was exhumed. No one was surprised when the poison was once more identified.

As the authorities continued their investigation, they charged Marie with attempting to murder Carol. On 11 November 1979, after being released on bail, Marie was driven to a Birmingham motel by her attorney, Wilford Lane. After a few days, she asked to be moved to another location. She feared the vengeance of Frank's sisters. Meanwhile, the condition of Frank's mother continued to decline. On 18 November, her body weakened by arsenic poisoning, she died. That same day, Wilford Lane discovered that his client had disappeared. Her motel room, which showed the signs of a minor struggle, contained a rather melodramatic note. 'Lane, you led me straight to her. You will hear from me.'

Less than 24 hours later, Marie's aunt arrived home to find that her house had been burgled. Clothes and a suitcase had been stolen and her car was missing. A note had been left at this scene, as well. The burglars – for the note clearly read 'we' – told her not to worry; they would not be bothering her further. It was clear to everybody that both notes had been written by Marie. She had fled, but where to was the question.

A NEW IDENTITY

It is known that she somehow managed to make her way to Fort Lauderdale, Florida, where in February of 1980, she met a shy, 33-year-old divorcee named John Homan. At 46 years of age, Marie was considerably older than Homan but she solved the problem by adopting a new identity. The multiple murderer now presented herself as Robbi Hannon, a 35-year-old Texan. Within a year, the couple had married and moved to Marlow, New Hampshire, where Marie found employment at the Central Screw Corporation. Her story was intriguing. 'Robbi' was a Texan heiress whose two children had perished in a horrible automobile accident. Her story became sadder still when she revealed that she was dying of a rare blood disorder. Robbi's search for a cure led her to consult a number of out of town specialists. John stayed behind on these occasions. Then in September 1982, Robbi made a trip for an entirely different purpose. Her twin sister Teri was experiencing marital problems, so she had to fly to Texas to provide support. Robbi Hannon Homan was never seen again.

As it happened, Marie ended up in Florida. She bleached her hair, became 'Teri Martin' and began working as a secretary for a man named Jack McKenzie. It was not long before Marie was telling her new boss about Robbi, her ailing twin sister. On 10 November, Marie telephoned John Homan. Introducing herself as Teri Martin she informed him that Robbi had died. On the following day, the surviving twin appeared in Marlow. 'Teri' was thinner than 'Robbi' had been – and she was blonde. Because of that she fooled many people, including her husband John, who welcomed her into his home.

However, some of the workers at the Central Screw Corporation were not so sure. Several of them were certain that Robbi and Teri were one and the same person. When

Teri placed an obituary for her deceased twin in the local paper they did some checking. They discovered that the hospital in which 'Robbi' had died did not exist, nor did the church at which her 'funeral' had taken place.

When they were presented with these findings, the local police investigated further. They came to the conclusion that Teri, or Robbi, might be a woman named Carol Manning, who was wanted for robbing a bank. However, on 12 January 1983, after being arrested at her place of work, 'Teri Martin' revealed that her true name was Audrey Marie Hilley. A week later, Marie was back in Anniston, where she was tried for Frank's murder, as well as the attempted murder of her daughter. When faced with the evidence, the defence really stood no chance. Marie was found guilty. She received a life sentence for Frank's murder, with an additional 20 years for poisoning Carol.

On 9 June 1983, she began serving her sentence as a medium security prisoner at Alabama's Tutwiler State Women's Prison. Incredibly, two years later Marie became classified as a minimum security prisoner, which made her eligible for day passes and periods of leave. By

19 February 1987, she had qualified for a three-day pass. That same weekend she met John Homan in an Anniston hotel room. Still smitten with the woman he had known as Robbi and Teri, he had been looking forward to spending a weekend with her. On Sunday morning, Marie left the hotel after telling John that she wished to visit her parents' graves. When she did not return, he went back to the hotel and found a note. 'I hope you will be able to forgive me,' it read. 'I'm getting ready to leave. It will be best for everybody. We'll be together again. Please give me an hour to get out of town.' Marie went on to say that she was flying to Canada and would contact him later.

But the fugitive never got there. On 26 February, four days after she had disappeared, Marie turned up in Blue Mountain, just a few minutes away. She was suffering from hypothermia and it was too late to revive her. Why was she there? Had somebody arranged to help her escape? Nobody knows.

KIMBERLY HRICKO
death after a
murder mystery

It was supposed to be a romantic getaway. Steve Hricko was making one last attempt to rekindle his dying marriage, so he had taken his wife Kim on a Valentine's Day weekend with a difference. The management at the luxurious Harbourtowne Golf Resort had organized a murder-mystery event. At the centre of the entertainment was a whodunit play. The guests enjoyed dinner while they watched the performance and then they all decided who had killed whom. But only two hours later the game would be played for real. One of the audience would be found murdered and all of the other guests would be called as witnesses.

The couple at the centre of the real-life mystery were Steve Hricko and his wife Kim. They had first met in

1984, after being introduced by mutual friends. Although Steve had been a football star in high school he was still a somewhat shy, reserved soul. Kim, on the other hand, was outgoing and lively. This marked difference in personalities did not seem to be important at the time. It was not long before the two married. The friends who had introduced the couple, Mike and Maureen Miller, served as best man and maid of honour at their wedding.

Steve was employed as golf course superintendent at a Baltimore country club, while Kim worked at the city's Suburban Hospital as a certified surgical technologist. They had one child, a girl named Anna, who was nine years old at the time of the murder. Nearly everyone, it seemed, thought they were a happy couple. However, nine years into their marriage, things were not going at all well. Although Steve did not know it, Kim had begun having an affair with a 23-year-old United States Marine Corps sergeant.

While he knew nothing about the affair, Steve had no illusions about his marriage. He began attending counselling in an effort to become more communicative, and he wrote his wife a lengthy letter about their problems. His wife later shared it with her friends, mocking him. As Valentine's Day approached, he asked Mike Miller to recommend a place where he and Kim might spend a romantic evening. His old best man went one better. He suggested that the couple spend the weekend at the Harbourtowne Golf Resort, where he worked. Mike even went so far as to make certain that Steve and Kim had one of the finest cottages the establishment had to offer. Steve's determination to save the marriage seemed only to irritate Kim. As she complained to one of her friends, 'He's smothering me and following me around the house like a puppy dog.'

OPTIMISTIC OUTLOOK

However, Steve saw things quite differently. On 9 February 1998, he made an optimistic entry in his journal. 'Life at home is improving and I am looking forward to Valentine's weekend at Harbourtowne with Kim... She called twice today and said "I love you" without [my] saying it first. I was very happy.'

On Valentine's Day, Kim and Steve started out on the 75-mile (120-kilometre) drive from their Laurel home to St Michaels – 'the Heart & Soul of the Chesapeake Bay' – a picturesque community that has become a favourite location for those looking for a romantic location in which to marry. The weekend package included the Valentine's Day dinner theatre staging of *The Bride Who Cried*, a whodunit in which a groom is poisoned at his own wedding reception. The guests of the resort were encouraged to take part in the hunt for the murderer. As it turned out, Kim was one of the more active participants. She followed the actors as they carried the 'murder victim' out of the ballroom.

The romantic weekend for the couples staying at the Harbourtowne Golf Resort ended in the early hours of Sunday, when Kim walked calmly into the lobby.

'I need to speak to someone who works here,' she said. 'I think my room is on fire.' When asked whether anyone might be inside, she replied, 'Yes, I think my husband is.'

A guest and a hotel employee raced across the resort's car park and entered the cottage. They found Steve lying on the floor, close to a *Playboy* magazine. His pyjamas were around his knees. The two men struggled to drag the golf course superintendent out of the room, only to discover that they were too late. Steve was dead – his upper torso and his head were burned beyond recognition.

According to Kim, she and Steve had returned to their cottage after the murder mystery, but when Steve had tried to pressure her into having sex they had argued.

Kim claimed that she had then driven off to visit Mike and Maureen Miller in Easton, some 6 miles (10 kilometres) away, but she had become lost. It was an unusual situation, because Kim had visited the Millers on several occasions. She had even driven to their home only ten weeks earlier. What made Kim's claim even more suspicious was the fact that her brother, to whom she was quite close, lived just a couple of streets from the Miller residence. And why had she not telephoned the Millers for directions? She had had her mobile with her.

After having been away for 90 minutes, Kim said, she had returned to the cottage to find it filled with smoke. Kim told the police that her husband had been drinking heavily – that he had been 'sloppy drunk' – yet his blood contained not a trace of alcohol. It seemed strange, therefore, that a number of empty beer cans were found in the room. A cigar, thought to have been the cause of the fire, added to the mystery. Kim claimed that Steve smoked, yet this was denied by his family and his friends. Perhaps more curious was the normal level of carbon monoxide in Steve's lungs, which indicated that he had died before the fire had started.

Phil Parker, the hotel guest who had dragged Steve out of the cottage remembered something unusual about Kim. 'All she kept saying was that she wanted to see his dead body. But I don't think anyone had told her he was dead.'

ODD BEHAVIOUR

At the funeral, five days later, several people noted Kim's odd behaviour. Indeed, the minister who conducted the service thought something was not quite right in the way she was acting. Then on 23 February, Kim's life as a free woman came to an end. The police arrived at the home of the friends with whom she had been staying. Armed with a search warrant, they began looking through her car. As they did so, the surgical assistant swallowed approximately 60 Xanex tablets and then threatened to kill herself by using a razor blade. She was subdued, charged with first-degree murder and arson and taken to a psychiatric hospital, where she was placed on suicide watch.

Kim's trial began on 10 January 1999 – it featured a parade of friends, neighbours and colleagues. Incredibly, the personable Kim had been quite open with everybody. She had been more than willing to discuss ways of murdering her husband with all and sundry.

Steve's death would be much better than a divorce, it seemed, because it would bring her and Anna a $450,000 life insurance payment. Kim had confided all of this to a neighbour. Then it was the turn of Jennifer Gowen, a colleague from the Suburban Hospital and the cousin of the man with whom she was having an affair. Jennifer testified that Kim had clearly told her that she wanted to kill her husband. Another colleague, Ken Burges, testified that two months before the murder Kim had asked him whether he knew of anyone who would kill her husband. She was offering $50,000 for the contract killing, he added. It became clear to Kim that she had asked the wrong person, so she told him to forget the whole conversation. Burges told the court that he was taken aback, but then he dismissed the conversation by making a flippant remark.

'You work in the operating room... You could just put him to sleep.'

The prosecution built on Ken's testimony by arguing that Kim had injected Steve with a muscle paralyzer known as Sustinalcolene, which she had access to through her work as a surgical technologist. Indeed, as Jennifer Gowen would testify, Kim had raised the idea of using the drug to kill Steve just a few weeks before the murder.

'We had a discussion about a case history where a woman had injected some children with Sustinalcolene and that that was a muscle relaxing anaesthesia agent and that it would go untraced.'

Further damning testimony came from Rachel McCoy, an old college friend with whom Kim had shared her plans for murdering Steve. The conversation, Rachel said, took place on 30 January 1998, 16 days before the murder.

'She told me that she could get a drug that would paralyze Steve, that would stop his breathing and then she would set the curtains on fire with a candle or a cigar and that he would die of smoke inhalation in a fire and nobody would know.'

Other evidence was presented. It was demonstrated that Kim, not Steve, had bought the cigars that were found in the cottage. However, tests revealed that the fire could not have been started by a cigar. All interesting, to be sure, but one suspects that Kim's own behaviour and words were more than enough to seal her fate.

On 15 January 1999, after a trial lasting only six days, Kimberly Hricko was found guilty of murder and arson. She was sentenced to life imprisonment.

ELENA KIEJLICHES
murder first,
then Disney World

Borys Kiejliches was a prosperous businessman, a Russian émigré who had become an American millionaire. But on 25 April 2000, his body was discovered stuffed in a barrel. It had been washed up in a marsh on the border between the New York City boroughs of Brooklyn and Queens. His head had been blown open by a single shot from a large-calibre pistol. The dead man's hands were well into decomposition, but it was apparent that they had been tied together. This was the first that anyone had seen of Borys in over a month.

Borys had been missing since 24 March 2000. Not that anyone thought to report the disappearance – at least not at first. Instead, his wife Elena chose to treat their two children, aged eight and five, to a trip to Disney World.

On 2 April, after her return from Florida, Elena made a drunken visit to the local Staten Island police station. She finally reported the fact that her husband was missing. Detective Steven Esposito would later recall the event. 'She was a little unsteady in her walking. I walked next to her so she wouldn't fall. Her speech was slurred. She looked dishevelled.'

Drunkenness aside, Elena's behaviour had been considered odd in many other ways. She had rocked back and forth, clutching her knees to her chest, and at one point she had curled up into a foetal position on the station floor.

A HISTORY TO HIDE

Elena said she had taken the children to Disney World on 24 March, after an argument with her husband. However, when the police asked her when she had returned, 36-year-old Elena was unable to provide an answer. After having reported her husband missing, Elena then became unco-operative. She refused to talk to the investigators, even though they were only trying to assist her at that point.

In view of what she had to hide, Elena's silence was not surprising. Eight years into her marriage to Borys, a man 15 years her senior, she had taken up with a man named Messiah Justice, a 25-year-old would-be rap musician. He had an arrest record that stretched back over a decade. The pair became entangled after a chance meeting at a red light in Manhattan. That is, their cars stopped at the same time. From this fleeting beginning they began an affair that lasted for some 18 months. Elena was nine years older than the rap musician. As the wife of a millionaire, she was able to shower her young lover with gifts: jewellery, clothes, shoes, mobile telephones and $85,000 in cash. Not only that, Messiah would stay at the Kiejliches mansion whenever Borys was away on business.

It did not take the police long to find out about the relationship between the émigré and Messiah Justice. When he was approached by the authorities, the aspiring rap star willingly testified at Elena's trial. Messiah described how his lover called him to the Kiejliches mansion on the evening of 24 March 2000. She met him at the door and led him downstairs. Her hands were covered with what appeared to be blood. There, on the floor of the mansion's finished basement, lay her husband's body, wrapped in sheets and tied with a cord.

According to Messiah, Elena told him not to worry. She said, 'You're not involved in this, and I'm going to take care of you, sweetie. But you have to help me. I'd help you.'

First of all he took the body to an abandoned building in Brooklyn and then he stuffed it into a barrel, which he dumped in Jamaica Bay. By this time, Elena and her two children were enjoying their Disney World holiday. They had left the day after the murder. Had she thought that she might distance herself from the crime through simple geography? If so, the plan had been poorly thought out. The timing of this impromptu trip was suspicious to say the least. Even more so when the telephone company's records indicated that Elena had made nearly 100 calls to Messiah over the course of her stay.

After her return to New York, Elena showed how much she appreciated Messiah's assistance – she made an

$8,000 down payment on a Bentley. Sadly, the cheque bounced. Elena's trial drew to a close on 25 June 2002. It took the jury just three hours to reach a guilty verdict.

NANCY KISSEL
poison in a
pink milkshake

Nancy and Robert Kissel moved in together shortly after they met in 1987. Two years later they married: the late AIDS activist Alison Gertz was maid of honour. At the time, Robert was studying for a master's degree in finance at New York University. Nancy had two degrees of her own – in business and design – but she took three humdrum jobs to support the household.

After graduating in 1991, Robert set out on a trajectory that would have brought him earnings of well over $3,000,000 a year within a decade. He began his dramatic rise in New York at the investment bank Lazard Frères, before moving on to the Goldman, Sachs Group. In 1997 he was transferred to Hong Kong. The Kissels then became prominent members of the American expatriate community. It should have been an enviable life – many outsiders thought it was. The Kissels and their two children settled into a luxurious suite at the exclusive Hong Kong Parkview. Robert worked and prospered, eventually joining Merrill Lynch, and Nancy did voluntary work. She assisted at the Hong Kong International School and the family's synagogue. In 1998, the couple were blessed with another child.

However, despite appearances Nancy would later claim that her years in Hong Kong had been extremely unhappy. If what she claimed was true then the SARS epidemic of 2003 was the answer to her prayers. In March of that year, Nancy and her children joined the stream of Americans who were fleeing Hong Kong for the relative safety of the United States. Leaving Robert to his work at Merrill Lynch, she travelled to the family's holiday home in the shadow of Stratton Mountain, Vermont. As the months passed and the epidemic worsened, Nancy decided to have an elaborate home theatre system installed. It was as a result of this desire for escapism that she met a twice-divorced electrical repairman named Michael Del Priore.

Before long, Nancy and Del Priore began having an affair. With Robert many thousands of miles away in Hong Kong they were able to enjoy much of the summer together. Nancy bought her lover a $5,000 wristwatch, which was perhaps an unusual possession for a man who lived in a trailer park. By August the SARS crisis had abated, so Nancy and the children were back in their Hong Kong Parkview suite. The marriage continued as normal, but Robert must have noticed a difference in his wife's behaviour.

Suspecting that his wife was having an affair, he hired a private investigator. It took little effort to uncover the relationship, yet no physical evidence could be obtained.

Shortly afterwards, Robert again contacted the private investigator. This time, though, he was asking for a bit of advice. The banker said he had recently drunk a glass of single malt scotch, but it had not tasted right. After a few sips he had felt 'woozy and disoriented'. The detective advised Robert to have a sample of the scotch analyzed, but the banker failed to do so.

Nancy became fearful that her husband was on to her. She hid her calls to Michael by getting her mobile phone bills sent to the Hong Kong International School. However, her caution was no match for her husband's determination. Robert had spy software installed on all of the family's computers so that he could monitor Nancy's email and Internet use. He saw that his wife had been using search engines for such terms as 'drug overdose', 'sleeping pills' and 'medication causing heart attack'. And yet, despite all these findings, Robert would not act. The most he did was tell his friend David Noh, a colleague at Merrill Lynch, that he was worried about being poisoned.

A COCKTAIL OF DRUGS

On 2 November, Andrew Tanzer, a Hong Kong Parkview neighbour, dropped his daughter off to play at the Kissels' suite. As he got ready to return to his home, Tanzer and Robert were offered pink-coloured milkshakes, which they both drank. By the time Tanzer returned to his suite he felt heavy with sleep, so he lay down on the couch. His wife was unable to rouse him for a while, though he later recovered somewhat. He drifted in and out of sleep until dinner time. Tanzer's behaviour then became even more unusual. First of all he appeared disorientated and then he acted in a childlike manner by displaying an almost insatiable appetite. Before falling asleep for the evening, he lost control of himself and soiled the furniture. On the following day, Tanzer found that he could remember next to nothing of what had taken place after he had left the Kissels' home.

Disturbing though Tanzer's experience had been, Robert Kissel's night had been much worse. When Andrew Tanzer woke up the next morning, the investment banker had been dead for many hours. The milkshake that the two men had drunk had been laced with six medications, five of which had been recently prescribed to Nancy. These were Stilnox, a sleeping pill; Amitryptaline, an antidepressant; Dextropropoxythene, a painkiller; Lorivan, a sedative; and Rohypnol, better known as the 'date rape drug'. Robert would have reacted to the concoction in much the same way as Andrew had. The difference was that Mrs Kissel had taken the opportunity to murder Robert while he was incapacitated.

At five o'clock in the afternoon, a tired and sleepy-sounding Robert spoke to David Noh in preparation for a company conference call. Though the event took place only 30 minutes later, Robert did not participate – it seems that he had forgotten all about it. Curiously, Robert was on the line to his secretary less than half an hour after missing the conference call. It was the last time anyone at Merrill Lynch heard from Robert. At some point in the evening of 2 November Nancy Kissel picked up an eight pound (3.6 kilograms) figurine and gave Robert five blows to the head. She hit him so hard that she cracked his skull wide open.

Robert's corpse remained in the suite for three days, though it was out of sight of the Kissel children. As it lay locked in the master bedroom, Nancy began spreading conflicting stories. She told a doctor that Robert had assaulted her on 2 November. A maid was shown injuries that he was supposed to have made. Robert was now staying in a hotel, she said. His disappearance was noticed almost immediately. David Noh was disturbed to discover that he was unable to contact the investment banker: Robert was not answering his phone. Another friend, Bryna O'Shea, was also worried. Aware of Robert's marital difficulties she had made calls to several hotels, thinking that he might have moved out of the Parkview. On 6 November, after comparing notes with Bryna, David notified the authorities.

CLOSING IN

Investigators interviewed Nancy at the Parkview apartment just a few hours later. It was her second contact with the police that day. That morning she had made a complaint against Robert. She had claimed that he had assaulted her five days earlier, when she had refused to have sex with him. Her weak attempt at creating a smoke screen had been in vain. The Parkview maintenance men had told the police that on the previous day Mrs Kissel had asked them to move an oriental rug to her storage locker. It had proved to be so heavy that four men had been required for the job. With this news, the investigators left the building to obtain a search warrant.

As midnight approached, the police entered the Parkview storage room. It took them next to no time to find Robert's corpse. As they suspected, it had been hidden within the rolled up rug, though not very well. Robert's remains had been sealed in two layers of plastic – and yet there was an omnipresent stench of death. Shortly before three o'clock in the morning, Nancy was arrested and charged with murdering her husband. Throughout all of her years in Hong Kong, Nancy had been immersed in the American expatriate community. Now she was going to have to face a jury that was composed entirely of ethnic Chinese.

The prosecution presented Nancy as an adulterous wife who had murdered her husband so that she could run off with her lover. The evidence against the widow Kissel was almost overwhelming: the prescription medicine that had been present in the milk shake; the testimony of Andrew Tanzer; and the rolled-up carpet that the maintenance men had moved to the storage room. Faced with these findings, and more, Nancy's solicitor fell back on British law. This allows the defendant to enter a plea of diminished responsibility if the circumstances surrounding the crime are extraordinary.

Nancy began testifying on 1 August 2005. It was then that she provided a detailed description of a man who was unrecognizable to the other American expatriates. She claimed that her husband had been addicted to cocaine, that he was an alcoholic and that he would beat her and force her to have oral and anal sex almost every single night. The sex had been so rough, she said, that Robert had once broken one of her ribs. Nancy then explained away her Internet research on sleeping pills, drug overdoses and medications that might cause heart attacks. She claimed that she had done it at a time when she had considered killing herself.

The blackening of Robert's character continued. Nancy told the court that her deceased husband had been a bad parent. When she had been pregnant with their youngest child, Robert had wanted labour to be induced so that the birth would not conflict with a business trip he had planned. At another point, he had become so angry with one of his daughters for playing loudly while he had been on the telephone that he had broken the girl's arm.

Nancy admitted to the affair with the Vermont repairman, though she claimed that she would never have left her husband. According to Nancy, the same could not be said for Robert. She told the court that on the day her husband had died he had stood in the doorway of the kitchen as she was making the pink milkshakes. While holding a baseball bat 'for protection', Robert had told his wife that he had filed for divorce. He also said that he would be taking the children, because Nancy was not fit to care for them.

Nancy then testified that she and her husband had begun to fight. She said that Robert had struck her and had then tried to rape her. The figurine had been grabbed in self-defence, but she had then hit him on the head with it. Robert had sat stunned but when Nancy had tried to help he would not let her. Instead, he had taken the baseball bat and swung it at her legs. At that point, she fell silent. She claimed that she could remember nothing more of the evening or of the days that followed.

The prosecution took issue with Nancy's testimony.

They asked her why she had never mentioned the abuse she had suffered to anyone, doctors included. And why was it that no one had seen any signs of injury? Nancy's story fell apart even more when the Kissel's maid testified that the broken arm had been nothing to do with Robert. Indeed, he had not even been home when the accident had occurred.

On the evening of 1 September 2005, the jury reached a unanimous decision – Nancy was found guilty of murder. Under Hong Kong law the mandatory sentence is life imprisonment. Because their mother has been found guilty of the murder of their father, the three Kissel children will one day inherit Robert Kissel's estate, which is estimated at 18 million dollars.

KATHERINE KNIGHT
the woman
who worked
in a slaughterhouse

Katherine Knight once worked in Australian slaughterhouses where she discovered a talent for decapitating pigs. She used the very same knives from her work to murder her common-law husband. John Price was skinned and beheaded; portions of his buttocks were cut from what remained of his body. All this was in preparation for a stew intended for his children. But it was not the work of a madwoman; courts determined that Katherine was quite sane. She had planned the murder, knew that it was wrong and was well aware of the consequences of her grisly actions.

Katherine Mary Knight was born on 24 October 1955

at Tenterfeld, New South Wales, one of many communities in which her father, Ken, had found work as a slaughterhouse worker. Kath lived a semi-transient life until 1969, when her family settled in Aberdeen, 170 miles (270 kilometres) north of Sydney. The town may have been small – with just over 1,500 inhabitants – but the Knight family was large. A twin, Kath was one of eight children.

VIOLENT BULLY

Barely literate, she wasn't much of a student; Kath still made a mark at the schools she attended by being a violent bully. At the age of 16, following in the footsteps of her father, brother and twin sister, Kath became a slaughterhouse worker herself. The following year, she met and moved in with David Kellett, a 22-year-old truck driver. The couple married in 1974, a happy occasion that was marred when the bride, disappointed by his sexual performance on their wedding night, tried to strangle her groom.

As the relationship progressed, so too did the abuse. In what, by comparison, seems a trivial incident, Kath burned all David's clothing. Early in the marriage, he arrived at work with the imprint of an iron burned on to the side of his face. The truck driver once awoke to find his wife astride his chest holding a knife to his throat. And yet, he stayed with Kath long enough to father, and witness the birth of, a daughter, Melissa, born in 1976. It was a joyous occasion in an otherwise unpleasant and disturbing period.

'I never raised a finger against her,' David said, 'not even in self-defence. I just walked away.' Within two months he had done just that, leaving his wife for another woman.

In retaliation, Kath placed Melissa on railway tracks just minutes before a train was scheduled to pass. The baby was discovered and saved by a local drifter, and, incredibly, the mother suffered no repercussions. Kath was not so lucky when, a few days later, she disfigured a 16-year-old girl's face with a butcher's knife. A stand-off ensued, during which Kath held a young boy hostage. She was placed in a psychiatric hospital, only to be released a few weeks later. There was a reunion with David, who worked to save what was left of the marriage.

DOOMED

The attempt was doomed from the start. Despite the medication and therapy she'd received, Kath was, if anything, more violent. And yet, in 1980 the couple had a second daughter, Natasha.

It would have been understandable had David again walked away, yet it was Kath who ended the relationship. He returned home one day to discover his house stripped of its contents and Kath, Melissa and Natasha gone.

In 1986, she began seeing a man named Dave Saunders, with whom she had a daughter, Sarah, the following year. Kath soon left her slaughterhouse job, citing a back injury. With Dave's help, and the aid of a significant compensation package, she bought a rundown house in an undesirable area of town, and, setting health concerns aside, began renovating and decorating. Kath's tastes were fairly unconventional: cow hides, steer horns, a stuffed baby deer, rusted animal traps and a scythe hung on a rope above her couch. And the pattern of her life was unchanged. Kath cut up her boyfriend's clothes, vandalized his car, hit him with an iron, stabbed him with scissors and

Jane Andrews and Tom Cressman shared a tempestuous and violent relationship

Tracie Andrews demonstrates the 'starey eyes' of the man she had invented as the scapegoat for the crime

Celeste Beard was given a life sentence for her role in the murder of her husband

Linda Shaw

Linda Shaw

The morbidly obese and ruthless Sue Basso in a police mugshot from August 1998

Lonely: Buddy's craving for female companionship ultimately cost him his life

Miami Herald

Rex

Joyce Cohen hid a calculating streak that nobody could have predicted

Betty Broderick during her trial

Adele Craven [right] upheld her innocence until the testimonies against her left her with no option but to confess

The Enquirer

Corbis

The scores of invented stories Evelyn Dick [left] fed to the police ultimately failed to cover her tracks

Nannie Doss's police mugshot [right], taken in Tulsa in October 1954

PA Photos

POLICE DEPT
TULSA OKLA
31486

Fairfax Media

Kathy Folbigg [left] admitted 'flashes of rage, resentment and hatred' towards her children

Tracey Frame [left] had believed that burning the body would prevent police from identifying it. She was wrong

Rita Gluzman [right] seemed part of a happy marriage until the relationship soured

Linda Shaw

Corbis

History repeats itself: Marie Hilley [left] was the second female killer to emerge from the tiny town of Blue Mountain

Kim Hricko's bubbly personality contrasted sharply with her man's reserved nature

Linda Shaw

Jupiter Entertainment

Seized: a handcuffed Elena Kiejliches pays the price for murder

PA Photos

Family support: Nancy Kissel and her relatives outside the Hong Kong High Court

Ann Kontz used her master's degree to obtain a good income which she spent on enhancing her looks

News Observer

Two of a kind: Shelly with Jimmy Michael – both filed for divorce from their respective partners

Pond life: it soon emerged that Shayne Lovera had had affairs with a number of men in Frog Alley

Tall tales: Sharee Miller [above] manipulated her lover into murder by creating stories of marital rape and abuse

PA Photos

In trouble: Shawna Nelson makes anxious eye contact with her attorney Kevin Stobel

PA Photos

Dorothea Puente [right] invented a variety of excuses to explain the foul stench that came from her property

PA Photos

Suspicious mind: Ron was a drunken and lascivious man, and Margaret Rudin [left] became convinced he was having an affair

PA Photos

Pamela Smart [right] is led out of Rockingham County Superior Court

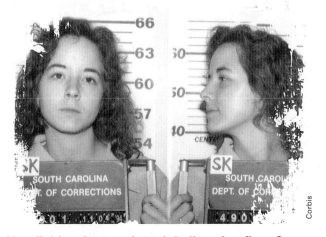

Unreliable witness: though believed at first, Susan Smith's interviews with the police revealed a number of inconsistencies

Out of control: Lynn Turner was an adulterer, an over-spender, and would ultimately become a murderer

Rosemary West grew up the daughter of a depressive mother and a violent schizophrenic father

beat him with a frying pan until he was unconscious. Even more disturbingly, Kath took one of Dave's dogs, an eight-week-old puppy, and, making certain he was watching, killed the creature by cutting its throat.

As their relationship drew to an end, Kath took an overdose of sleeping pills and wound up in another psychiatric hospital. And yet, she managed to obtain an Apprehended Violence Order that kept Dave away from her and his child.

By May of 1990, Kath had moved on to another man. John Chillington, a cab driver, became another victim of her abuse. She smashed glasses grabbed from his face and destroyed his false teeth. Despite the drama, in 1991 the pair had a child, Eric, together.

In 1994, Kath dumped John for her final partner. John Charles Price, known as 'Pricey'. He was a well-liked man; even his former wife, with whom he'd had four children, spoke of him only in glowing terms.

After a little more than a year together, Kath abandoned her shoddy, bizarrely decorated home for Pricey's more tasteful, well-built bungalow. Even before moving in, the relationship had taken several bad turns. The pair had been seen fighting – typical behaviour for Kath, but very much out of character for Pricey.

Frustrated by Pricey's refusal to marry her, Kath presented a video tape to her boyfriend's employers depicting items allegedly stolen from his work. Though the goods featured, all well-past their expiry dates, were probably scavenged from the trash, Pricey was fired – an abrupt end to 17 years of dedicated service.

Kath and Pricey split up. But within a few months were back together.

Unable to read or write, Pricey's employment options were extremely limited. Pricey sunk into drink for a time, until, by chance, he happened upon a job at Bowditch and Partners Earth Moving. It was just the sort of break he needed. A year after being hired, Pricey was made supervisor.

He'd begun to share elements of his unhealthy relationship with the boys from work, telling them that Kath had a history of violence and that he wanted her out of the house. Pricey also claimed his wife could throw a punch as good as any man alive and that she'd once chased him with a knife. Pricey's stories were at odds with the woman known to his friends at work. The Kath they'd seen might have been a bit of an odd bird, but to an outsider she seemed pleasant enough.

By the early months of 2000, Pricey had begun making an effort to share his concerns.

On 21 February, he was forced to flee the house after Kath had grabbed a knife in an argument. Though some of Pricey's friends encouraged him to leave, he felt the need to stay in order to protect the children. Eight days later, during his noon-hour break, Pricey went to a local magistrate. He feared for his life and showed a wound he'd received when Kath had stabbed him. After returning to work, his boss offered him a place to stay, but Pricey declined.

FAMILY VIDEO

A family video, shot just a few hours later, captures Katherine singing nursery rhymes to her children. Her sole grandchild, a girl, sits on her lap. It was an out-of-character performance, complete with the peculiar message: 'I love all my children and I hope to see them again.' After the camera was switched off, she and the children enjoyed a dinner at a local Chinese restaurant. Again, it was something out of the ordinary. Kath told the children, 'I want it to be special.'

Aged twenty, Natasha had a vague feeling of unease about the meaning of her mother's unusual behaviour. As Kath left to see Pricey, she said, 'I hope you are not going to kill Pricey and yourself.'

Later, Kath claimed that she had no recollection of the evening after having watched *Star Trek* at Pricey's house. Much of what we now know is drawn from forensic evidence gathered at the scene. We know that at some point Kath donned a black negligee bought at a local charity shop. It's highly probable that she was wearing the flimsy garment when they had sex – it is certain that Kath had on the negligee when she began stabbing Pricey. The wounded man managed to make it outside his front door before being dragged back into the house, where the stabbing continued. The coroner determined that

Pricey received at least 37 stab wounds, destroying nearly all of his major organs.

When Kath began skinning, beheading and otherwise carving up her lover is unknown, though cameras did manage to record her movements at 2.30am, when she made a withdrawal from an ATM.

It was at Bowditch and Partners that the first concerns for Pricey were raised. Such was Pricey's dedication and reliability that at 7.45am his boss phoned local police to report that he had not yet arrived at work.

The authorities visited Pricey's bungalow, forced the door and found his skin hanging in a doorway. The decapitated corpse was lying in the living room. Pricey's head was in a large pot, simmering away on the kitchen stove.

The dining room table held two servings of food, consisting of baked potato, pumpkin, courgette, cabbage, squash and generous portions of the cooked corpse. Placement cards indicated that the two settings were intended for Pricey's children. Barely literate notes containing baseless allegations were addressed to the children.

Having taken a mild overdose, the author, Kath, lay semi-comatose on the bed she and Pricey had once shared.

In October 2001, Kath admitted her guilt in Pricey's death. The following month she became the first woman in Australia to receive a life sentence without the possibility of parole. Speculation remains as to whether she ate any of the meal prepared from Pricey's body.

ANN MILLER KONTZ
killing a husband,
losing a lover

Ann Brier, later Ann Miller Kontz, was born in Batavia, New York, but she was raised in comfort in the Pennsylvania town of Spring Grove. She met Eric Miller at Purdue University when she was 18 years old. They were immediately drawn to each other, partly because they were both highly intelligent, dedicated chemistry students. But romance did not prevent them from working hard at their studies. In 1992, they both graduated with master's degrees in biochemistry. With their degrees finally under their belts they got married in that same year.

Still ambitious, they continued their studies at North Carolina State University. This time they were both enrolled on PhD courses. In 1998, Eric obtained his PhD, but instead of taking one of the high-paying jobs offered by the pharmaceutical industry he obtained a federal grant to do research into paediatric AIDS. Although Ann was perfectly capable of emulating Eric's success, her studies were interrupted in January 2000, when she gave birth to Clare. Motherhood and a PhD course did not mix, so she abandoned that particular route. Instead, she used her master's degree to obtain a well-paid position as a research scientist with GlaxoSmithKline, one of the top pharmaceutical companies in the country.

Eric and Ann had shared many ideals as students, but they began to drift apart. Ann now spent a good portion of her income on beauty treatments and cosmetic surgery, while Eric focused his attention on his research. Not only that – Ann also began spending more and more time with her colleagues. On 15 November 2000, she encouraged Eric to meet up with her new male friends for a 'guys' night out'. They all went off to a local bowling alley, where they shared hot dogs and beer before the game. Eric thought the food was fine, but he said the beer tasted strange. One of Ann's colleagues put it down to the fact that beer was never any good in bowling alleys. As it turned out, Eric did not finish his drink because he accidentally spilled it. It was a clumsy move that might very well have bought him a few more weeks of life.

After the group had played a few frames, Eric experienced severe stomach pains. Food poisoning, everyone thought. But as the evening progressed, Eric's condition deteriorated dramatically. Before midnight, Ann drove her husband to the Rex Hospital. The stricken man was given myriad tests, but nothing could shed any light on the nature of his condition. With Ann by his side, Eric stayed at the hospital until 24 November, by which time his condition seemed to have improved. When he was released, he went back home to Ann and their daughter.

HALLUCINATIONS

However, six days later Eric doubled up in pain shortly after eating dinner. Ann then drove him back to the hospital, where he began hallucinating. He was thrashing about so much that he had to be placed in restraints. By chance, he was in this state when the results of his earlier tests came in. They showed that there had been an extremely high level of arsenic in Eric's system. The only possible conclusion was that Eric was being intentionally poisoned.

The Raleigh Police Department was notified and its officers quickly arrived on the scene. However, it was too late. At approximately two o'clock in the morning, Eric died of arsenic poisoning. The evidence showed that the scientist had been receiving small regular doses of arsenic during the five months leading up to his death. Everything pointed to Ann. After all, who but Eric's wife had the opportunity to administer the repeated doses of poison? On 4 December, two days after Eric's death, police executed a search warrant at GlaxoSmithKline. First of all, they found 200 millilitres of sodium cacodylate, a toxic arsenic compound. Just as interesting, Ann's email records showed that she had been having affairs with a number of men, including a married colleague named Derril Willard.

Things quickly came into focus for the investigators. After interviewing those present on the November 'guys' night out' at the bowling alley, they learned that Derril had bought Eric's beer. He had even poured the drink for his lover's husband. On the morning of 21 January 2001, police arrived at Derril's house, armed with a search warrant. As the investigators combed through his house, Ann's lover was taken aside by Chris Morgan, a Raleigh police detective. Morgan told Derril that it was his opinion that he had been used by Ann. According to the detective, Derril looked up and responded, 'Yeah, and she did a good job of it.' With that, Derril told Morgan that he would say no more. He wanted his lawyer.

Less than 24 hours later, Derril committed suicide by shooting himself in the head. The dead man left behind a wife and a daughter. There was also a note in which he apologized to his family and denied any involvement in Eric's death. His widow, Yvette, was allowed little time to grieve before the Raleigh Police Department turned up on her doorstep. She told the investigators that Derril had admitted to the affair, but had denied any involvement in Eric's murder. And yet her husband had consulted a lawyer, Richard Gammon, who had told him that he could be charged with attempted murder.

After learning about the lawyer's opinion, the investigators were certain that the conversation between Gammon and the dead man contained important information. Accordingly, they asked for a transcript of what had been said. However, Gammon refused to co-operate, citing attorney–client privilege. That was the beginning of a legal tussle between the two parties.

It all came to an end in May 2004, when the North Carolina Supreme Court ruled that the attorney had to reveal the contents of his conversation with Derril.

Much time had passed, during which Ann and her daughter Clare had moved to Wilmington. There she had met Paul Martin Kontz, a Christian rock musician. The couple had married in November 2003. And yet, despite all the delay, the information that had been obtained from the dead man's lawyer became an important part of a grand jury investigation into Eric's murder. Entered as 'Exhibit A', it related to Eric's hospital stay in late

November. Part of it is quoted here.

> Mr Willard then stated that on one recent occasion he had met Mrs Miller in a parking lot, and they had a conversation while in an SUV. He stated that during this conversation Mrs Miller was crying and that she told him she had been in the hospital where Mr Miller had been admitted. She stated to Mr Willard that she was by herself in the room with Mr Miller for a period of time. She then told Mr Willard that she took a syringe and needle from her purse and injected the contents of the syringe into Mr Miller's IV.

There would be no trial. In November of 2005, nearly five years after Eric's death, Ann settled for a plea deal in which she admitted to conspiracy to commit first degree murder and a reduced charge of second degree murder. She was handed a sentence of 25 to 31 and a half years' imprisonment.

Ann's lawyer read a statement in which she said that she felt 'a deep sense of remorse and regret' over the murder.

SHAYNE LOVERA
cheating in
Frog Alley

Alicia Shayne Good, known as Shayne, did not have an easy beginning in life. Born in 1966 to teenage parents, the first years of her life were spent in poverty. Things became no easier when her parents split up. Then, in 1973, Shayne's life changed beyond recognition. Her mother, now divorced, married a high-profile bank president. A move to the Gatlinburg, Tennessee home of her new stepfather quickly followed.

Suddenly, at the age of seven, Shayne was thrust into a lifestyle that at first seemed very foreign to her. Surrounded by luxury, she wanted for nothing.

Shayne had only just begun her studies at a Missouri university when she met a fellow student named Kelly

Lovera. A year afterwards, in 1986, they were married. Five years and two children later, Shayne urged Kelly to move to Tennessee, so that she could be closer to her family.

The couple settled in the city of Sevierville, some 13 miles (20 kilometres) to the north of Gatlinburg. However, the geographical proximity in no way meant a return to the life of privilege that Shayne had once enjoyed. Their cramped, rented one-storey townhouse, in an unattractive neighbourhood called Frog Alley, was a far cry from her stepfather's luxurious home.

MONEY PROBLEMS

Since getting married, Shayne had been finding it difficult to adjust to her new, more modest lifestyle. She spent money that the couple didn't have, racking up debt that would take years to repay. As Shayne shopped, Kelly concentrated his efforts on earning a master's degree in mathematics so that he could 5 November 1994, Shayne held an outdoor barbecue at their townhouse complex. It turned into a wild evening of drinking and gambling, so it was not the sort of evening that would appeal to everyone. Indeed, one of the very first to leave the party was Kelly. It was the last time anyone there would see him alive.

Next morning, a pair of tourists driving through the Great Smoky Mountains National Park came upon a sight that was not found in any travel guide. In the valley below the road on which they were travelling, just 33 feet (10 metres) away, lay a black Jeep. Inside the vehicle sat the lifeless body of Kelly Lovera. At first, it appeared that the tourists had stumbled upon the scene of an accident – the vehicle had gone off the road and hit a tree head on. However, a casual inspection revealed something peculiar. Although the Jeep was pointing downhill, blood had been dripping from the back of the vehicle.

Kelly's injuries also raised the suspicions of the authorities. Part of an ear was missing and it appeared that he had been severely beaten about the head. It was all inconsistent with the injuries one would expect from an otherwise straightforward crash. The Sevier County Sheriff's Department began to think that Kelly had been murdered. Shayne told the police that she had last seen Kelly at about 4.30 in the morning. It had been an unpleasant parting – they had been arguing and he had stormed off. There was little in Shayne's story that satisfied the investigators so the sheriff's department decided to obtain a search warrant for the townhouse. However, before they did, a man walked into the station to report that a friend had just given a lift to a man named Brett Rae.

It seemed that the 26-year-old Rae, a Frog Alley neighbour of the Loveras, had admitted to running Kelly off the embankment.

BLOODY TRAIL

On 8 November, two days after the murder, the police returned to the Lovera townhouse, this time armed with a search warrant. The investigators could see that somebody had attempted to clean up some blood stains, but they had a range of techniques at their disposal. With the aid of luminol, a chemical that is used to detect tiny amounts of blood at crime scenes, they discovered a bloody trail that began at the couch. There was a drag pattern along the hallway and out through the children's bedroom window. That was enough for the detectives.

On 13 November, Shayne was arrested and charged with the first degree murder of her husband. Brett Rae was also arrested. The pair would be tried together. In both cases, the state sought a sentence of life without parole.

In the subsequent trial, the prosecution asserted that Shayne and Brett were lovers. They had acted together in killing Kelly. After the murder, Shayne had begun cleaning the townhouse up, while Brett had driven Kelly's remains into the Great Smoky Mountains National Park. But things went wrong. Although Brett had intended to push the Jeep over the side of a mountain, with Kelly at the wheel, it had hit a tree. Brett refused to testify on his own behalf and he would not implicate Shayne. Undeterred, the prosecution turned to one of the pair's neighbours, a young man named Wade Hill.

It soon emerged that Shayne had been having affairs with a number of men in Frog Alley, Wade included. Wade testified that Shayne had spoken to him about killing her husband. She had even speculated about the best type of poison to use. At the time, Wade said, he had taken her words as a joke.

After Wade had left the stand, Shayne chose to testify. She told the court that Brett had committed the murder alone. He had killed her husband during a fight that had been fuelled by Kelly's jealousy. According to Shayne, Brett had stopped by the apartment to talk to her when he was confronted by Kelly. The two men had begun fighting in the small living room.

At some point, Brett had picked up a baseball bat. He had only intended to keep her husband at bay, but Kelly had been accidentally struck. When he fell back on to the couch Brett realized that he was dead. All of this had taken place while she was asleep in the bedroom, Kelly said. She heard nothing of the fight. In short, she knew nothing of what had really happened.

Certain that she was convincing the court, Shayne went on. Not only had she had nothing to do with her husband's death, she was not even Brett's lover. They were, she said, nothing more than neighbours. What Shayne did not know is that when she and Brett had been out on bail they had been followed by a member of the Siever County Sheriff's Department. One day, Shayne and Brett were followed into the mountains, where they were spotted having sex amongst the trees. Confronted by this evidence, Shayne told the court that she had consented to sex with Brett after he had threatened to implicate her in the murder.

'My purpose in going there was trying to save what little bit of a life I had left at that point', she testified.

On 28 March, after only 90 minutes of deliberation, the jury handed down two verdicts. Both defendants were guilty of murder in the first degree. Faced by the inevitable, the lovers changed their respective pleas to guilty.

By promising not to appeal, they would each have the opportunity to request parole after serving 25 years.

JESSICA McCORD
a boot full of
burning bodies

For Alan Bates, life seemed to progress at a rapid pace. In 1990, at the age of only 20, he had married Jessica, his high school girlfriend. The bride had been pregnant at the time. Just months after their honeymoon, the young couple were joined by a healthy baby girl, who was named Gabrielle. A few months later, Alan moved the family to Montevallo, Alabama, 40 minutes south of Birmingham, where he was going to attend university on a theatre scholarship. Three years later, a second daughter, Madeleine, was born. By 1993, the couple had bought a house in Montevallo – quite an achievement for a couple in their mid-twenties. Then came the marriage breakup.

SETTLEMENT

In 1995, Alan and Jessica's divorce became final. Jessica was granted custody of the girls and she was given the couple's Montevallo home as part of the settlement. All was fairly cordial at first – that is, until Alan began dating again. Then in 1999 he remarried. His new bride, Terra was an art historian. Jessica did not take kindly to the idea of her daughters having a stepmother. Even though Alan was granted visitation rights and daily telephone calls, Jessica soon found ways of blocking his access to the children. She lied about the girls' whereabouts, she cut visits short and she stopped answering the telephone. Not content with all of that, she even removed her mailbox.

Finally, Jessica moved out of the house without informing Alan. Some time passed before he was able to track his daughters down.

Jessica made no effort to hide her animosity towards her ex-husband. She told the girls' dance instructor that Alan would regret it if he ever tried to gain custody. Jessica's aggressive behaviour continued even after Alan and Terra moved to Frederick, Maryland, where they took jobs with a local theatre company.

Even though Jessica had not been content to leave the past behind, it seems that she had moved on in her romantic life. One relationship had resulted in the birth of a child.

And now she had a new partner – a police officer named Jeff McCord. The couple had met at the Birmingham Police Department, where Jessica was employed as an administrative assistant. It was a good job – so good that she held on to it even when Jeff was transferred to suburban Pelham.

In June 2000, Jessica and Jeff were married. It was a happy occasion in what was otherwise a very difficult year. Jessica seemed to be unable to control herself where her ex-husband was concerned. After assaulting Alan and being absent without leave, she was fired from her job at the Birmingham Police Department. In his termination notice, the chief of police wrote these words: 'You went to the home of your ex-husband and you admitted you hurt him to keep him from hurting you.'

Later that same year, Jessica was found in contempt of court after she failed to show up for a custody hearing. She was jailed for ten days. Then in November Alan came back from Maryland to request that his wife be again declared in contempt of court – this time for denying him access to his daughters. The policeman's wife devoted a lot of time and energy to making sure that Alan did not see his daughters. She dodged subpoenas, changed addresses and transferred Gabrielle and Madeleine from school to school. But the law managed to catch up with her. In December 2001 she was found guilty of violating a series of court orders that went back 15 months. She was sentenced to ten days in a Shelby County jail. 'Somebody is going to pay for this,' was her response.

PLOTTING MURDER

Jessica devoted much of her time in jail to devising ways of murdering her ex-husband and his wife. 'What if I kill them, put them in a trunk of a car and run it in the river?' she asked a fellow inmate. 'Do you think I'd get away with it?'

While the courts had been a source of much frustration to Alan, it seemed that things were beginning to improve at the beginning of 2002. On 15 February, he and Terra flew to Birmingham for yet another appearance before a judge. This particular trip was meant to have at least an element of pleasure. They had made arrangements to take Alan's daughters to his parents in Atlanta for the weekend. After renting a car they went to Jeff and Jessica's home to pick up the girls. A little over nine hours later, a farmer dialled 911 to report what he believed was a forest fire. In fact, the flames he saw were coming from a burning rental car. The bodies of Alan and Terra were found in the boot. They were riddled with bullets and burned beyond recognition.

The police investigation focused on Jessica from the start. Her hatred for her ex-husband was well-known. Indeed, it had been documented in several child custody hearings and in her notice of dismissal from the Birmingham Police Department. So Jessica and Jeff were interviewed and their house was searched. But then they disappeared. The police continued the investigation in their absence. Fortunately, an important clue was soon found at the crime scene. It had seemed so insignificant at first. What could have been less interesting than a piece of kitchen roll? As it turned out, it was the brand and style that was later found in the McCords' kitchen. It appeared that the paper towel had been used to set the car on fire.

A further search of the couple's home revealed what appeared to be a sloppy repair to a wall. Behind the damage, police found a bullet. According to ballistics it had been fired from the gun that had been used to murder Alan and Terra. After a few days the McCords were found to be staying with relatives in Florida. They did return eventually, but not before Jeff was fired from his police job after failing to show up for a disciplinary hearing.

On 21 February 2002, a mere five days after the bodies had been found, Jessica and Jeff were arrested and charged with the murders of Alan and Terra Bates. The couple were tried separately. Then on 16 February 2003, exactly a year after the bodies had been found, Jessica was convicted of the double homicide. She was sentenced to life imprisonment with no chance of parole. Two months later, Jeff pleaded guilty to the murders. He was also sentenced to life imprisonment. It was through his testimony that the authorities were able to put together a timeline.

FALLING INTO THE TRAP

According to Jeff, Alan and Terra had arrived at their home at dinner time, with the intention of picking up the girls for the weekend. What the couple did not know was that Gabrielle and Madeleine were not at the McCord home. Instead, they were staying with Jessica's mother. The former police officer described how he and his wife had lured Alan and Terra into the house with a handwritten note taped to the front door. 'Come to the back,' it read. 'We're having trouble with the front door.' There had, of course, been nothing wrong with the door. The pair did as they were asked and went round to the back of the modest split-level house. They passed a sign which read, 'PROUD TO BE AN AMERICAN,' and then they entered through the back door. There was nobody around, so they sat down on a couch while they waited for the girls. Then Jeff opened fire. He pumped four bullets into each of the seated figures.

After stuffing the couple's bodies into the trunk, Jeff took the wheel of their rental car and drove nearly 250 miles (400 kilometres), a trip lasting four hours, with Jessica following in their own car. He exited the highway at Morgan County. The choice was made quite by chance. Any rural location would have done – any place where Jeff and Jessica would not have been seen. They set the car on fire and then returned home. It was dawn when Jessica and Jeff finally got back. It had been a very long night. Yet both of them knew that they could not postpone cleaning the crime scene up. Together they removed the blood-soaked upholstery from the couch. Ever the handyman, Jeff went the extra distance and replaced some floor tiles. But the couple were less than thorough. They overlooked traces of Terra's blood on a glass coffee table. And then, of course, there was that bullet that they had left sealed in the wall.

Jeff will be eligible for parole in 2033, after making a

deal in which he agreed to testify in any other trials arising from the case. He later assisted in the prosecution of his mother-in-law, Dian Bailey, who had perjured herself during Jessica's trial.

SHELLY MICHAEL
burning down
the house

Michelle Goots, known as Shelly, was a popular girl by any standards. As well as being very intelligent she was also a cheerleader and a high school athlete. A straight-A student who went on to university, she stood out in the small West Virginia town of Clarksburg. And yet for all her intelligence, Shelly went on to commit a very obvious murder in her adult years.

Shelly's relationships with men seemed to be a hindrance to her progress in life. As a very young woman, her studies at West Virginia University were interrupted when she became pregnant by a fellow student. By the time the baby was born, however, she and the father were no longer a couple. In 1994 Shelly, now a single mother, returned to school, but it was not long before she met

Rob Angus. They got married and had a daughter, which delayed Shelly's studies yet again.

It was not until 1997, more than six years after she had first attended classes at West Virginia, that Shelly finally received her degree.

After graduating, Shelly got a job at the university's Ruby Memorial Hospital in Morgantown. She also developed a reputation for being a bit of a flirt. Among those who received her attentions was repertory therapist Jimmy Michael. That Jimmy was married – to another therapist, Stephanie Estel, who worked in the very same hospital – appeared to be of no consequence. By the autumn of 1998, it had become obvious to Stephanie that her husband was having an affair. In the following year, Shelly and Jimmy filed for divorce from their respective spouses. They married in May 2000, three months after Jimmy's divorce was made final. The newlyweds then bought a house just a five-minute drive from the hospital.

It seemed that things could not be better. Jimmy left the hospital to start Mountaineer Home Medical, a successful medical supply business and Shelly returned to the university on a part-time basis. After obtaining her master's degree she became a nurse practitioner. They were seen by many, Jimmy's parents included, as something of a perfect couple. In their leisure time, Jimmy would coach Pee Wee football while his wife would drill the cheerleaders.

On 29 November 2005, the perfect couple was no more. Shortly after 10.30 in the morning, Shelly received an urgent call at the hospital. Her house was on fire.

The nurse rushed over to see the second storey of the building in flames. After a half-hour battle, the local fire fighters managed to douse the inferno. It was only then that they made an awful discovery. Jimmy's remains were lying on what was left of the marital bed.

NO EMOTION

From the start, the investigators could sense that something was not quite right. Shelly's behaviour, for a start. While it was to be expected that she would have raced over from the hospital, her subsequent behaviour started to look odd. She displayed less emotion than the average bystander. Indeed, according to some witnesses Shelly displayed no emotion whatsoever – there were no tears. Jimmy's remains also seemed very unusual. The investigators noticed that the dead man looked as if he had simply been asleep. He was lying flat on his back and he appeared to have made no effort to escape the inferno.

Three days later, the medical examiner discovered that Jimmy had no smoke in his lungs. The Pee Wee football coach had been dead before the house fire even began. It was clear to the police that Jimmy had been murdered. Morgantown had a population of less than 30,000, so homicide was big news. Rumour and speculation were rampant, not least concerning the dead man's 33-year-old widow. The police had received an anonymous tip that Shelly had committed the murder with the aid of a drug.

And the results of the toxicology tests revealed that there was indeed a deadly drug present in Jimmy's remains.

Jimmy might have been the perfect husband, but Shelly had not been anything like the perfect wife. On 7 December, the questioning of Bobby Teets, one of Jimmy's employees, brought an admission. Bobby revealed that he had been having an affair with Shelly. It had started, Bobby said, in a Chicago hotel room, and it had continued right up to the day on which Jimmy was found dead. Indeed, only three days earlier Bobby and Shelly had enjoyed sex on the very bed in which Jimmy's remains had been found.

When they had finished with Bobby, the investigators turned again to Shelly. They began by asking her to describe her relationship with Bobby. 'Just friends – but good friends,' the widow replied. Then they asked her about the morning of the fire. Shelly had maintained that she had been at work when Jimmy had died. Indeed, hospital records and video surveillance show this to be true. But those same video recordings showed the nurse leaving the hospital at 8.11am. She would not return for 17 minutes.

Armed with this knowledge, the investigators told Shelly what they had discovered. She immediately changed her story. This time she told the detectives that she had left the building to retrieve a pager from her SUV. Then she was told that a video recording showed her driving the vehicle out of the car park. Again she changed her story. 'No, I didn't leave the hospital,' she said. 'It was raining really hard, so I was gonna move my car to the garage.' Finally, the interrogating detective played the trump card. In a sworn deposition a neighbour had said that she had spotted Shelly pulling out of her driveway at around 8.15 to 8.20am on the morning of the fire.

At this point Shelly became visibly upset. 'I lied to you about going to the house,' she admitted. 'And I've had to live with the guilt of not noticing anything was wrong – if there was something wrong at the time.'

On 6 February 2006, four months after the murder, the toxicology report was finally presented to the investigators. The document indicated that at the time of his death Jimmy's body contained a lethal amount of the neuromuscular blocker rocuronium. Typically used in surgery, injections of the drug are always accompanied by the use of a ventilator.

To do otherwise would lead to a very slow suffocation. As a nurse, Shelly had easy access to both the drug and the ventilators through her work at the Ruby Memorial

Hospital. However, it seems that on the morning of 29 November 2005 she used one without the other.

Four days after they had received the toxicology report, members of the Morgantown Police Department went to the apartment that Shelly had rented after the fire. The widow was arrested and charged with murder and arson. Shelly was granted bail on condition that she did not leave her parents' Clarksburg home. However, she did herself no favours by ignoring the court's instructions. She was spotted running errands and she even visited a salon to have her nails done. Breaking bail cost her a month in jail.

Shelly was then photographed giving a 'thumbs up' sign as she entered the courtroom on the first day of her trial. The prosecution argued that she had injected Jimmy with rocuronium in order to benefit from his $500,000 life insurance policy while continuing her affair with Bobby. The timeline presented by the prosecution suggested that Shelly had injected her husband before leaving for work. Once at the hospital, she had then worked to establish her alibi by making her rounds. The nurse was confident that she would not be missed in the 17 minutes it would take her to drive home, start the fire and return to the hospital.

SLOW BURN

The defence did not deny that Shelly had returned to the house. Instead it focused on the two hours that had elapsed between her brief return home and the time at which the fire was first reported. It was argued that the fire could not have smouldered for two hours before being noticed. In fact, testing by arson experts from the Bureau of Alcohol, Tobacco, Firearms and Explosives proved otherwise.

Shelly took the stand in her own defence. She told the jury of six women and six men that she loved her husband. Jimmy had been killed, Shelly said, but she was not the murderer. When the prosecution suggested that she had lied to the police over 100 times in their investigation, Shelly did not deny the fact. 'I lied a lot,' she conceded. She then tried to suggest that Jimmy had committed suicide by first injecting himself with rocuronium and then setting his bed on fire.

Despite her best efforts Shelly was found guilty of murder and arson on 20 July 2006. The murder conviction alone carried an automatic life sentence.

SHAREE MILLER
instant messaging
murder

J **erry Cassaday spent nine years of his short life** as a sheriff's deputy in Cass County, Missouri. For a time he did quite well. His skills and qualities were recognized and he became a lieutenant.

However, by 1994 the job had begun to sour so Jerry resigned from the force. Life, it seemed, was on a downward spiral. His marriage broke up and he was abusing drugs and alcohol.

Several years passed before Jerry finally managed to grab the reins and begin turning his life around. Then in 1998 he got a job working in security at Harrah's North Kansas City Casino and Hotel. The following July found the former police officer working at the chain's casino in Reno, Nevada.

It was there that he met a vivacious blonde named

Sharee Miller. She was married, but that did not seem to be much of an obstacle.

Sharee had not been Mrs Miller for very long – just a few months, in fact. Her husband, Bruce, 20 years her senior, was a worker at General Motors. On the side, he owned an auto salvage business. Though she was just 27 years old, Sharee's marriage to Bruce was not her first, nor was it her second – Bruce was her third husband. They lived in Flint, Michigan, together with three children from Sharee's previous marriages.

After years of hardship, the new bride was now living the sort of comfortable lifestyle that had previously eluded her. The home Sharee shared with her new husband, while not luxurious, was a far cry from the trailer in which she had grown up. However, she showed she had a reckless streak by obtaining a number of credit cards and running each of them up to their limits.

ADULT CHAT ROOM

Bruce was a hard worker, a trait that Sharee seemed to have picked up. She became a Mary Kay beauty consultant. Hours were spent on the computer each day, supposedly in an effort to grow her business. Trips down to Reno became a frequent thing. In reality, though, Sharee's computer time was devoted to corresponding with Jerry.

The pair had met through an adult chat room – Sharee went by the name of 'iwanttobelaid'.

The business trips were nothing more than clandestine meetings with her lover. Despite the distance, the relationship between the pair moved at a rapid pace. They began to talk of marriage and starting a new family together. In September, two months after their first meeting, Sharee told Jerry that she was pregnant with his child. It was only a matter of time before they would be starting a new life together. The only obstacle, it seemed, was Bruce.

On 23 September 1999, Sharee transformed the hard-working auto worker into a fictional character that neither he nor anyone else would have recognized. Corresponding through AOL Instant Messages, Sharee informed her boyfriend that she had suffered a miscarriage.

'This next part will be hard – I lost my baby, Jerry.'

'No.'

'I never thought I would ever tell you that he [Bruce] hits. I got in trouble because I was with you.'

Over the course of the messaging, Jerry asked where exactly Bruce had hit her.

At first, Sharee appeared reluctant to share the information, but she eventually relented.

'He didn't hit me, Jerry; he raped me – I lost the baby because of the force.'

For Jerry, the news was devastating – almost too much to bear. On the following day he told Sharee how bad he felt.

'No one, I mean no one, is going to get away with the things he has done to you.'

When he told Sharee to leave her husband and go to

live with him, she responded that Bruce would never let it happen. He was, she claimed, a powerful person in the world of organized crime. According to Sharee, her husband was involved in drug trafficking and money laundering. As if it needed saying, she added that he was a man capable of violence.

Incredibly, the very next month, Sharee announced that she was again pregnant. Jerry, it seemed, would be the father of twins. She sent her lover sonograms of their two babies over the internet. Jerry was ecstatic. However, on 5 November, within days of the happy news, Jerry's mood underwent another dramatic shift when he received an email that was addressed from Bruce's account. It began:

'Sharee is growing fat with two bastards in her. She has decided she doesn't like the excess weight and is going to get an abortion.'

Frantic with grief, Jerry made a desperate attempt to contact his lover, but he only met with failure. More than a day passed before he heard from Sharee. There was no telephone call, just a brief email.

'This is Sharee. I am going away for a few days. I will contact you next week sometime.'

Another day passed. Then Jerry received a second email from Bruce's account.

'Well, Jerry, she told me to let you know she would be home soon. I think the abortion went fine. She sounded like she felt better knowing she wasn't having any more kids... Thank you for making my relationship with my wife better.'

Hours later, Jerry received an email from Sharee. She had sent him several disturbing photographs of herself. It appeared that she had been beaten. He knew that Bruce had to die. In the early hours of 8 November, the former sheriff's deputy and his girlfriend used instant messaging to plan the murder.

'Jerry, don't look at him, don't talk to him.'

'Don't worry.'

'You yourself said to me.'

'I know.'

'That if I looked at him, or talked then I couldn't do it.'

'He will beg.'

'But that is different I don't know him.'

'And you know it. Just do it and get the hell out of there.'

'I want him to know who I am.'

'Jerry, please.'

'He will not know for long.'

A few hours later, Jerry got into his car and drove the 11 hours from his home in Odessa, Missouri to Bruce's auto salvage yard. It was a trip made easier by Sharee, who had provided directions. She had even told him which roads to take in order to avoid encountering the police. After making good time he arrived at about 6.30pm. As it happened, Bruce was still in his office. This fitted in well with Sharee's plan. She had told Jerry that it was better to kill her husband indoors because the sound would carry less. The auto worker was on the phone to Sharee, talking about getting a takeaway pizza. He hung up as Jerry made his way into the office.

The one-time sheriff's deputy aimed his .20 calibre shotgun at Bruce and said, 'Hi, I'm Jerry.' With that, Sharee's lover pulled the trigger, killing Bruce instantly. He then got into his car and drove home. But it was almost as if the shotgun blast had also killed the stream of electronic correspondence between Sharee and Jerry. The smitten casino worker continued to write, but more often than not he was met by silence.

After a couple of weeks, Sharee told him that their relationship was over. This was true enough – two weeks after Bruce had been killed, she had moved in with another man.

THE BODY

Bruce's body was discovered by his brother and his sister-in-law. Sharee had called them after her husband had failed to return home from work. Initially, the police believed that the whole thing was a robbery that had gone wrong.

After all, the assailant appeared to have taken the dead

man's wallet and Bruce was known to carry very sizeable amounts of cash around. The authorities zeroed in on John Hutchinson, a former employee who had been in trouble with the police on several occasions. He also owed Bruce several thousand dollars. Hutchinson had no alibi for the evening – surely, he must have done it.

Yet the police also kept an eye on the widow. Upon being told of her husband's murder, Sharee had demonstrated understandable shock and grief. However, two days later, she had been spotted dancing and simulating sex at a bar in Otisville, about 18 miles (30 kilometres) outside Flint. Even so, the investigation was progressing rather slowly – but it would soon get a shot of adrenalin.

SUICIDE NOTES

On 11 February 2000 Jerry sat in his recliner. It overlooked the small lake that bordered his nondescript Odessa apartment building. With an open Bible on his lap, he pushed the muzzle of a .22 calibre rifle into his mouth and pulled the trigger. He left behind a number of suicide notes, including one addressed to his parents that read:

I was so blind and so stupid and so much in love. She just wanted all her money and no more husband... I know it was all just more lies and games from Sharee. She didn't care what it took or who she hurt to get what she wanted.

Jerry's next note was directed towards his brother. The dead Jerry asked his brother to retrieve a briefcase that was located under his bed. He was to take it to John P O'Connor, a Kansas City lawyer Jerry had once met.

When O'Connor opened the case, he found that it contained transcripts of the electronic correspondence between Sharee and Jerry. The police were to uncover even more evidence on the hard drive of Jerry's computer. It was clear to the police that Sharee had plotted her husband's murder. On 22 February 2000 she was arrested and charged with conspiracy and murder in the first degree.

Sharee's trial began on 13 December 2000. From the start, the prosecution was able to demonstrate the subtle ways in which Sharee had manipulated Jerry. The lovelorn casino worker had been led to believe that she was married to a dangerous, abusive man. Not only that, Sharee had also managed to convince him that she was carrying his babies. In fact, it would not have been possible. Sharee had opted for a tubal legation after the birth of her third child. The procedure had taken place well before she met Bruce, never mind Jerry. The sonogram pictures were not hers at all. If Jerry had only studied them carefully, he would have seen that they dated from 1994.

The defence argued that the police came to the right conclusion at the very start of their investigation. Bruce had been murdered by his former employee John Hutchinson. They also suggested that Sharee's lies had been aimed at scaring Jerry off, leaving her free to work on her marriage to Bruce. However, there was too much evidence stacked up against her.

On 23 December 2000, after two days of deliberation, the jury found Sharee Miller guilty of conspiracy and second degree murder. A month later she was sentenced to life imprisonment. She will not be eligible for parole until 2055, at which point she will be 84 years old.

In April of 2008, Sharee married husband number four, a 56-year-old man named Michael Denoyer who had contacted her after watching a report of her case on television.

SHAWNA NELSON
grim reaper
with a gun

Shawna Nelson was born in Colorado in 1971. At 18, she graduated from high school and took a job as a 911 dispatcher in Weld County, dealing with emergency telephone calls from members of the public. Shawna found the work exciting from the start and she quickly developed friendships with some of the people around her. Among her closest friends was Michelle Moore, a young sheriff's deputy.

Shawna spent so much time with her colleagues that it was no surprise when she began dating a sheriff's deputy named Ken Nelson in 1995. The couple married in the following year. Within months, the newlyweds were expecting their first child. Even though another child followed shortly afterwards, Shawna kept her job as a dispatcher.

In 2004, Weld County merged its 911 services with the town of Greeley, so Shawna was brought into contact with a whole new group of police officers. One of those she met was a detective named Ignacio Garraus. It was not too long before word got around that Shawna and Ignacio, a married man, were having an affair. Both of them had previously been involved in extramarital relationships, but this time it was different. Shawna sought Ignacio's wife Heather out, wherever she was, and then verbally abused her, using words like 'bitch'. This left Ignacio in an uncomfortable position. He covered himself by telling his wife that Shawna was simply a person who had an unhealthy crush on him. There was nothing more to the relationship, he said.

By January 2005, though, Ken Nelson had discovered that his wife had been cheating on him.

It was not long before he filed for divorce. The case was still pending when Shawna learned that she was pregnant with Ignacio's child. By that time it was July. The news came as something of a shock to Ignacio, who told the dispatch operator that he did not want her to have the baby. Shawna, on the other hand, was violently opposed to having an abortion. The affair had come to a sudden and unexpected halt.

With Ignacio no longer in the picture, Shawna turned back to Ken in an attempt to save the marriage. He put a halt to the divorce proceedings and agreed to raise the child as if it were his own. Then in March 2006 Shawna gave birth to a boy, who was named Christian. But as it turned out, the break with Ignacio had only been temporary. Shawna and Ignacio soon resumed their bedroom habits as if nothing had happened.

Meanwhile, things had begun to go wrong in the Garraus household. It all started when Shawna told Heather that Christian had been fathered by Ignacio. The police detective denied it at first, but on 16 December 2006 he decided to tell his wife the truth about the affair. He also owned up to the fact that he had fathered a child with the 911 dispatcher.

Heather immediately walked out of the door, but she returned the next day. She said that she wanted to make an attempt to save their marriage. Ignacio picked up the telephone and told Shawna something that she had not expected to hear. The police detective told her that Heather knew of the affair – he had told her himself – and then he added, 'You and I are done.' It seemed that this time Ignacio was serious. He accepted Heather's demands – a test for sexually transmitted diseases and marriage counselling. His wife presented him with a card in which she had written:

Ig,
As much as I am hurting, I want you to realize that I know
you are hurting too. It will take time and a lot of hard work.
I want to fight for us and I hope that everyday you see my face
you will see the HOPE!
I do Love you.
Heather

The couple took their only child, a daughter, off to Florida for Christmas. Heather hoped that the trip would mark a new start for their marriage. After they returned, Ignacio and Heather had their lawyer send Shawna a

letter requesting that she keep her distance. Heather then began receiving a number of threatening voice and email messages. One, dated 8 January 2007, is typical: 'Anytime anywhere bitch'. Another, sent to both Ignacio and his wife, featured a photograph of Christian, with the words, 'Ig's flesh and blood'. One message written to Ignacio alone read:

> I see why you're doing this now.... I'm the best lover you ever had AND the most loyal woman ever to be in your life... It all makes sense to me now why you would chose [sic] the other life filled with vanilla and FAT!

Heather was employed at the Greeley branch of the Credit Union of Colorado. On 23 January, a few weeks into the onslaught, she had come to the end of her working day and was looking forward to getting home. However, as she was walking through the car park with her colleagues, a black shrouded figure wearing a grim reaper mask stepped up to the group. Pointing a gun at Heather, the individual exclaimed, 'You... you've ruined my life.'

Heather was then forced to her knees before being shot twice in the head. She died instantly.

GRIM REAPINGS

The attacker had long fled by the time the police arrived on the scene, but this did not matter as far as Heather's colleagues were concerned. The shroud and the mask had fooled no one – they knew it was Shawna who had killed Heather. They had also seen the Nelsons' black Ford F250 pickup truck. Ken was at work when the news came through that his wife was being sought as a murder suspect. He sped off in his Jeep, hoping to find Shawna at home. En route, Ken spotted her in his rearview mirror and had her pull over. Other law enforcement officers were soon at the scene and Shawna was arrested. A search of the pickup truck revealed the grim reaper mask, hidden beneath a seat.

Ken would later face evidence-tampering charges. Witnesses at the scene had reported that the sheriff's deputy had removed something from the truck his wife had been driving. While these allegations were later dismissed due to insufficient admissible evidence, the murder weapon was never found.

Shawna's taped interrogation began within two hours of the murder. The suspect did not deny that she had been in the Credit Union of Colorado car park at the time of the attack, but she said that she did not know who had been murdered. Shawna was charged with first degree murder in what seemed like a simple, if bizarre, crime. However, in November, as the trial date drew near, the prosecution was forced to ask for a postponement. Michelle Moore had come forward to say that she and Shawna had planned the murder. Faced with this revelation, the authorities arrested and charged Michelle with conspiracy to commit murder. The sheriff's deputy accepted a deal that offered a maximum nine-year sentence in exchange for testifying against her friend.

THE EVIDENCE

When the trial finally began on 21 February 2008, things did not look too good for Shawna. Several pieces of evidence were presented that tied the accused to the murder. The killer's disguise had been found hidden in the truck she had been driving, a mere 15 minutes after Heather had been shot; tyre tracks found in the slush of the car park were a perfect match for the Nelsons' pickup; the shoes that the murderer had been wearing matched those of Shawna; and her hands, face and clothing tested positive for gunshot residue. A forensic investigator discovered that the two shell casings that had been recovered from the scene of the crime had been fired by a .40 calibre Glock handgun, the very gun that Ken Nelson had once given his wife as a gift.

Many of the members of Shawna's job-related social circle testified against her. A former colleague told the court that Shawna would visit the local shooting range and pretend that the target was Heather. Ignacio took the stand during the presentation of the threatening messages that his former lover had sent to his wife. The police detective testified that Shawna had placed seven calls to the Credit Union of Colorado on the night before the murder.

Much was made of the unusual manner in which

Shawna was dressed at the time of her arrest. She was wearing her husband's dirty clothing and a baseball cap and she had no shoes on. And this was in January, when there was snow on the ground. However, the police later found a pair of shoes. They were lying on the road along which Shawna had been driving when she had been stopped by her husband. Both of the shoes held traces of gunpowder residue and they looked like the shoes that had been worn by the killer.

As if this was not bad enough, the prosecution's case was bolstered by Michelle's testimony. The former sheriff's deputy told the court that Shawna had talked about driving to Heather's workplace so that she could shoot her rival. According to Michelle, on the night before the murder Shawna had said that she had to get rid of Heather.

Seven days passed before the defence was given its chance to respond. It argued that the Greeley police were so familiar with the affair between Shawna and Ignacio that they had been hasty in their judgement. In short, the department had failed to consider any other suspects.

Shawna's defence counsel put some questions before the court.

> Did Ignacio Garraus have a motive to get rid of both Heather Garraus and Shawna Nelson out of his life for financial reasons or for some other reason? I don't know. It wasn't investigated. Did Michelle Moore have a motive to get back at Shawna Nelson?

In order to answer the second question, Shawna took the stand. She told of a conversation that had occurred on the day before the shooting.

> I was driving Michelle home and told her that I no longer could have a sexual relationship with her, that I'd been thinking all through our drinks, and that since I was actually trying to finally be loyal to Ken, that I was going to go home and tell Ken about my relationship with her.

Ignacio, it appeared, had not been the only police officer with whom Shawna had been conducting an affair.

If this was true, it was something quite different from what Michelle had described as 'sisterly love' between the women. After this bombshell had been dropped, the defence argued that it was entirely possible that Michelle had killed Heather and had then framed Shawna for the crime.

The jury would have none of it. On 3 March 2008, after five hours of deliberation, the six women and six men returned a verdict of murder in the first degree. Shawna was stone-faced when she received the verdict and then she shook her head dismissively. She was sentenced to life without parole.

Heather's murder had been horrible by any standards. But the truth might have been even more diabolical than the jury had realized. Prosecutor Cliff Riedel has suggested that Shawna might have been wearing Ken's dirty clothing as part of an attempt to frame her husband. This might explain the disguise and her use of Ken's pickup. Had Shawna not been stopped by her husband the physical evidence might have suggested that Ken was the killer. If this imagined plot had come to fruition, the former 911 dispatcher would have eliminated Ken and Heather, which would have allowed her to live with Ignacio.

DOROTHEA PUENTE
bodies in
the garden

Dorothea Puente ran the prettiest of boarding houses in Sacramento, California. The two-storey gingerbread Victorian house was situated at 1426 F Street, a lush, tree-lined thoroughfare in what had once been a grand neighbourhood. Dorothea's house stood out proudly from the others, which had fallen into disrepair. She took great pride in the look of her home. It was decorated with lace doilies and a variety of knick-knacks. The 59-year-old Dorothea also paid a great deal of attention to her own appearance. She spent a sizeable amount of money on silk chiffon dresses, Giorgio Armani perfume and at least one facelift.

PRIM AND PROPER

Dorothea lived an orderly life, which was reflected in her orderly boarding house. Boarders lived on the ground floor, while Dorothea had the spacious second floor to herself. It was all quite proper. Her guests paid $350 per month. In exchange they received a private room and two very generous meals each day. If there was anything amiss it was the foul stench that appeared to be coming from her property. During the summer months the neighbours would complain to Dorothea. She would then come up with all sorts of excuses: the sewer was blocked up; rats were to blame; she had been using a fish emulsion to fertilize her back garden.

She tried to eliminate the smell, or at least cover it up, by dumping a quantity of lime and gallon after gallon of bleach on to her back garden. The boarding house itself was sprayed constantly with air freshener. When three police officers came to call on the morning of 11 November 1988, she had perhaps already sprayed her house. They were looking for one of her boarders, a 51-year-old mentally disabled man named Alvaro

Montoya. It was not that Alvaro was in trouble with the law – he just seemed to have vanished. His social worker was most concerned.

While Alvaro's room did not provide any clues as to his whereabouts, the officers noticed something unusual in Dorothea's back garden. In one corner of the property it appeared that the ground had been recently disturbed. Using shovels and spades, the three men began digging. Finally, they uncovered clothing and the remains of a human body. No one expressed more shock at the discovery than Dorothea.

Officials from the coroner's office arrived, as did a team of forensic anthropologists, supported by a work crew. Together, they worked to uncover the corpse. It appeared that the police officers had found the skeleton of a short female with grey hair. But that wasn't all. As the excavation continued, a second set of remains was uncovered – and these were much fresher.

MORE CADAVERS

Just after this gruesome discovery had been made,

Dorothea asked the detective in charge, John Cabrera, whether she might be permitted to go for coffee at the Clarion Hotel, just two blocks away. There was no problem with this request. After all, the boarding house owner was not under arrest. The detective did Dorothea the courtesy of escorting her through the gathered onlookers and then he returned to the garden.

As the afternoon progressed, the body count increased. Three more cadavers were found underneath a slab of concrete and another body had been buried beneath a gazebo. In the end, seven corpses – three male and four female – were found in Dorothea's back garden.

It went without saying that Dorothea would have to be questioned about the bodies that had been unearthed on her property. The only problem was that Dorothea had disappeared. She had never returned from her trip to the Clarion Hotel. Despite Dorothea's absence, a picture began to emerge. A note found in her quarters served as the key to what had been taking place. On this small piece of paper was written Alvaro's first initial, followed by those of six former boarders. Each of the initials was accompanied by a number, which was preceded by a dollar sign. The investigators had found a list of Social Security and disability benefits. Dorothea had been collecting money that had been intended for people who were dead. She became richer by $5,000 each and every month.

As they searched for the boarding house owner, the authorities began looking into her background. What they found was not pretty. She had been born Dorothea Helen Gray in Redlands, California, on 9 January 1929. Both of her parents had died by the time she was nine – her mother in a horrible motorcycle accident – and she was sent to a number of homes. As a teenager, she turned to prostitution. She was able to earn a fair amount of money from her good looks.

UNHAPPY UNION

Not long after the end of the Second World War, Dorothea met a 22-year-old soldier named Fred McFaul. They married in Reno. Though the couple had two daughters, their union was not a happy one. Dorothea lived an unrealistic fantasy life that required expensive clothing and evenings out.

She told people that she was the sister of the American ambassador to Sweden and that she counted Rita Hayworth among her closest friends.

In the midst of this fantasy life, she left her husband and daughters for the excitement of Los Angeles. There she became pregnant by another man. Though she miscarried, McFaul would not take her back. With the marriage at an end, their children were raised by others. Then in 1948, Dorothea served her first jail sentence. She was locked up for a total of four years after forging a number of cheques. Almost as soon as she was released, Dorothea wed for a second time. Though the marriage lasted for some 14 years, it was another disaster. It is likely that it only endured as long as it did because her husband, a merchant seaman, was often away.

Dorothea carried on working as a prostitute during both her marriages and in 1960 she was convicted of residing in a brothel. In 1968, she married for a third time. Her groom, Robert Jose Puente, was just over half

Dorothea's age. A year later, the marriage was over. As the 1970s began, Dorothea started to run the boarding house on F Street. After a few years, she ended up marrying one of her boarders, a 52-year-old named Pedro Angel Montalvo. The couple had not been married long when Dorothea was again arrested for cheque forgery. This time she avoided prison. She got away with five years' probation for the crime.

It is thought by the authorities that she committed her first murder in 1982. The victim, Ruth Munroe, made the mistake of starting a small lunchroom business with Dorothea. This happy, optimistic woman died from an overdose of codeine and Tylenol, a tragedy that the coroner dismissed as suicide. A mere month later, Dorothea was charged with drugging her boarders so that she could steal their more pricey possessions. It was a simple and obvious crime. As a result, she served three years in the California Institution for Women. Upon her release, Dorothea was told not to handle government cheques and to keep away from senior citizens. She violated both orders.

Still officially married to her fourth husband, the 56-year-old Dorothea became engaged to Everson Gillmouth, a man 21 years her senior. His body was found a few months later by fishermen who had been trying their luck in the Sacramento River.

ATTRACTING CUSTOM

By this point, Dorothea had returned to running her boarding house. A string of social workers favoured her with boarders. They were oblivious to her lengthy criminal record. In the words of one of their number, Dorothea had the 'best the system had to offer'. She was willing to accept into her boarding house the most difficult people that they had to place. However, she did not rely entirely on social workers for boarders. Dressed to the nines, Dorothea frequented the lesser bars of Sacramento. There she made conversation with lonely, down-and-out people, in a bid to encourage them to take a room at her boarding house.

All of these revelations came much too late. By November 1988 the authorities knew that they had to find Dorothea. But where was she?

BOGUS STORY

The investigators were later able to piece together just what had happened. After Detective Cabrera had escorted her to the Clarion Hotel, Dorothea had spent some time in a bar on the other side of town. She had then boarded a bus for Los Angeles, where she had met a 59-year-old carpenter named Charles Willgues in a tavern. She gave him a fake name and an equally bogus story – a cab driver had driven off with her suitcases. Dorothea tried to play upon the man's sympathy, but she did not get very far. When she suggested that they move in together, the carpenter declined. Later, in his apartment, Charles realized the true identity of the woman to whom he had been speaking. It was then that he called the police.

She was arrested the day after the bodies began to be pulled out of the ground. The former prostitute was later charged with nine counts of murder. It would take four years before Dorothea's case was ready to go to trial.

Her defence was extremely weak. Dorothea explained that the people whose bodies had been found in her back garden had all died of natural causes. She had buried them herself in order to hide the fact that she was operating a boarding house in violation of her parole. However, Dorothea's claims about natural deaths were countered by the concentrations of Dalmane, a prescription-strength sleeping pill, that were present in every one of the remains.

A friend of Alvaro Montoya took the stand to say that the dead man had complained that Dorothea had been plying him with drugs. The testimony of other witnesses indicated that the boarding house owner had been forcing drugs on her lodgers.

Dorothea was eventually found guilty on three counts of murder.

On 10 December 1993, she was sentenced to life imprisonment without the possibility of parole.

MARGARET RUDIN
the case of the
shattered skull

To my Fiduciaries:

I request that in the event my death is caused by violent means (for example, gunshot, knife or a violent automobile accident), extraordinary steps be taken in investigating the true cause of death. Should said death be caused, directly or indirectly, by a beneficiary of my estate, said beneficiary shall be totally excluded from my estate and/or any trusts I may have in existence.

These words come from a secret directive. They were not the product of a paranoid, but of a realist. Ron Rudin, the man who signed this document would indeed die a violent death.

Ron was a very wealthy man. He had made millions

out of real estate in and around the Las Vegas area. His wife, Margaret, an attractive blue-eyed blonde, was a barber's daughter. She had been born – but not raised – in Memphis, Tennessee. Indeed, before she had reached the age of majority, she had called 15 states her home. Her transient lifestyle seemed to be in keeping with her attitude to affairs of the heart. By the time 44-year-old Margaret had married Ron, in 1987, she had already been through four marriages.

TWO OF A KIND

However 50-year-old Ron had an identical track record. He too had had four previous marriages. One wife had even committed suicide. Margaret and Ron met through their church, the First Church of Religious Science in Las Vegas. They walked down the aisle of a local chapel together just three months later. Margaret's fifth marriage came at the end of a trying twelve months during which she had divorced her fourth husband, undergone a hysterectomy and suffered the loss of her father. But somehow she thought that her fifth marriage would solve most of her problems. However, her optimism quickly dissipated. Now married to a man she had known for only a few months, Margaret wondered if she had made a mistake. Ron's business dealings were seen as questionable and Margaret's diary entries portrayed a man who would look for any excuse to get drunk and flirt with other women. His luxurious Las Vegas home was small consolation to her.

Margaret was not alone in being unhappy with the union. In September 1988, after less than a year of marriage, Ron sued for divorce, only to withdraw the action eight months later. He had given incompatibility as the reason. Margaret then came to believe that Ron was having an affair with a woman named Sue Lyons, a former employee. She went so far as to bug his office phone. Copious notes were made of each and every conversation, no matter how trivial.

On 17 December 1994, Ron met Sue and told her that he thought he was being poisoned. Sue had problems of her own, although hers were not life-threatening. Her teenage children had received anonymous letters telling them that their mother was having an affair with Ron:

> *Your mother has been screwing Ronald Rudin the realter*
> *[sic] for over a year. She meets him at vacant houses he owns*
> *— during her work time — and she screws him on dirty carpet*
> *floors. He brags to his friends and laughs at her because he*
> *tells everyone he does not get a motel and he does not have*
> *to buy her a lunch...*

Sue was certain the letters had been sent by Margaret. She pointed out that one of them was addressed to 'Melissa Lyles' – but there was no Melissa Lyles. There was, however, a Natalie Lyles, whom Margaret had mistakenly called Melissa. Soon afterwards, Ron vanished.

MISSING HUSBAND

Two days passed before Margaret troubled herself to report her husband missing. It took an employee of his real estate company to convince her to go to the police. A few weeks later, his Cadillac was found behind the Crazy Horse Too Gentlemen's Club, an expensive, though by no means exclusive Las Vegas strip joint. Muddied and bloodied, the vehicle was anything but clean.

On 21 January 1995, Ron's body – or what was left of it – was found by three fishermen at Nelson's Landing on Lake Mohave, roughly 62 miles (100 kilometres) southeast of Las Vegas. The developer had been set alight in a fire pit, so there was little to see but a few charred bones. However, his skull displayed the clear evidence of four .22 calibre bullet wounds. A man's bracelet with 'RON' spelt out in diamonds had been found nearby, together with the remnants of an antique trunk. There was a funeral – but Margaret didn't attend.

The investigation into Ron's murder came together very slowly. It appeared that there had been no witnesses, though some fairly interesting evidence was found in the couple's bedroom. The walls and ceiling were stained with splattered blood and it appeared that a labourer had been called in to remove a number of blood-stained items, including a mattress and a carpet.

On 21 July 1996, more than a year after Ron's body was found, a scuba diver located a Ruger semi-automatic pistol belonging to Ron wrapped in a plastic bag beneath Lake Mead. Curiously, the dead man had reported it missing in 1988, at the time that he had taken steps to divorce Margaret. Ron was an avid collector of guns and he took considerable care with his firearms. The disappearance of the weapon was doubly mysterious, therefore. He told several friends that the only possible explanation could be that Margaret had taken the missing gun.

What was of even greater interest to investigators was the fact that ballistics tests showed that the Ruger had been used in the murder.

In the meantime, Ron's directive to his fiduciaries had come to haunt Margaret. As a suspect, she was cut out of his will. A subsequent civil action ended when the widow agreed to settle for $600,000, just over a twentieth of his £11million estate.

The amount only just covered her legal expenses. Then on 18 April 1997, the authorities were confident that enough evidence had been amassed to arrest, charge and convict Margaret for the murder of her millionaire husband. However, the police were unaware that

Margaret had left Las Vegas some weeks earlier, never to return. Or so she thought.

BLACK WIG

Margaret lived in Chicago, where she had relatives, for a short period of time. She took to wearing a black wig and she hid her blue eyes behind brown contact lenses. It is thought that she next lived in Phoenix, where she worked in a hotel gift shop. Incredibly, Margaret was almost caught when a colleague recognized her from a feature on the television show *America's Most Wanted*. The authorities picked up the bewigged murder suspect in August of 1998, but they released her when they were unable to obtain positive identification.

After that lucky escape Margaret quit Phoenix. She travelled light, because she left her clothing, make-up and other personal effects in a rented room at the YMCA. This time she crossed the border into Mexico. After living for a few months in Guadalajara, she clearly felt luck was on her side because she risked the keen eyes of US Customs and Immigration by returning to the United States.

Where she went next is anyone's guess. However, it is certain that she ended up in Revere, Massachusetts, a working-class suburb of Boston situated on the Atlantic coast. She had a new man in her life, a retired fireman named Joseph Lundergren. They lived together, but for once Margaret did not get married. Lundergren knew little of Margaret's past – and much of what she had told him was a lie anyway. For example, she said her husband had been killed by an Israeli terrorist called Yehuda.

TRACKED DOWN

Interestingly, it was another call to *America's Most Wanted* that finally brought Margaret down. She was apprehended after having been recognized by yet another viewer. In November of 1999, police stormed the small, rundown apartment she shared with Lundergren. They found Margaret hiding in the bathroom. 'This is about Las Vegas, isn't it?' she said. The suspect was flown 2,700 miles (4,400 kilometres) back to Las Vegas for trial. She described the flight as a 'liberating experience'.

On 2 March 2001, Margaret finally had her day in

court. The prosecution portrayed her husband as a man living on borrowed time. Margaret had attempted to kill Ron several years earlier, they said.

In April 1991, she had overheard a telephone conversation in which Ron had complained that he was not getting enough sex. Angered by what she had heard, Margaret pointed a gun at Ron. He went to grab it and there was a shot. The bullet missed Ron but damaged a painting in their bedroom. Not long after that near miss Ron had his lawyer draft the secret directive to his fiduciaries.

The prosecution then asserted that the antique trunk that had been found near Ron Rudin's body had been sold to Margaret some months before. There was also an attempt to implicate Yehuda Sharon, a former Israeli intelligence officer who had helped Margaret after the murder – or so the prosecution claimed. But although Sharon was offered immunity from prosecution, he steadfastly denied any knowledge of the murder.

THE MEN IN HER LIFE

Margaret's defence attorneys, on the other hand, criticized the police for not investigating the possibility that Ron had been killed by a business partner with a grudge. Margaret said that she had known about Ron's affair, but had accepted it. 'You know why?' she asked one journalist who interviewed her at about the time of the trial. 'It's because 99 per cent of the men that I've ever had in my life had affairs. Ninety per cent of men do; you might as well expect it.'

On 2 May, after five days of deliberations, Margaret was found guilty of murdering her husband and illegally wire-tapping his office phone. It was not until 31 August that Margaret received her sentence – life imprisonment with the possibility of parole after 20 years. She is currently held at the Nevada State Women's Penitentiary.

'I don't have a history of staying with somebody if I'm really unhappy,' Margaret once said. 'I have a history of divorcing.'

A court found that this was not always the case.

PAMELA SMART
murder on
Misty Morning Lane

Throughout the spring and summer of 1990, the thoughts and prayers of Derry, New Hampshire focused on a young woman named Pamela Smart.

The attractive and popular high school volunteer seemed to have suffered the greatest of tragedies. On the first day of May, Pam had arrived home to find Gregory, her husband of little more than a year, lying dead with a bullet in his skull. Blood was seeping from his wound on to the living room carpet.

At the time, Pam ran from neighbour to neighbour, pounding on doors and screaming for help, which was understandable. But as the days went by the 22-year-old widow had appeared stoic and composed – strong even.

It was these qualities that led the Derry Police Department to make Pam the primary suspect in the murder of her husband.

Although they both grew up in Derry, a town of less than 32,000, Pam and Greg Smart did not meet until the final day of 1986, when they both attended a New Year's Eve party. They had much in common, including an abiding love of heavy metal music. Indeed, as the 'Maiden of Metal', Pam hosted the weekly Metal Madness show for her university radio station. It was not long before they became a couple and began to talk of marriage.

BEGINNINGS OF DOUBT

Their chosen home, a two-storey townhouse on Misty Morning Lane, just three blocks from the groom's parents, at first seemed at odds with the couple's lifestyle – but Greg had begun to change. He got a job as a salesman with his father's insurance company, he cut his shoulder-length hair and he began to speak of his wife as a good mother for their future children. A dog was added to their little family, which Pam named Halen, after the rock band

Van Halen. Married life with Greg was secure but Pam felt a sense of great disappointment. Greg had all but given up the guitar, had taken to wearing suits and his interest in heavy metal was on the wane. Much worse than all of that, the 'Maiden of Metal' was shocked and humiliated when Greg admitted to having had a one-night stand with another woman. This was before the couple had even reached their first anniversary. It was an indiscretion for which Greg would never be forgiven.

As her husband settled into a comfortable career selling insurance, Pam began to set her sights considerably higher. Her dream was to build upon the communications degree she had earned from Florida State University and become a media figure on a par with Barbara Walters. However, Derry was not New York, Los Angeles, or even Tallahassee, the site of her Alma Mater. The opportunities she dreamed of just were not there. Two months into their marriage, Pam had managed to get a job as director of media services at a local school board. With the job came her own secretary and a dedicated 15-year-old student intern named Cecelia Pierce, who was always at her beck and call.

Pam sought to raise her professional profile by becoming an adult volunteer in Project Self-Esteem, a drug awareness programme. It was based at Winnacunnet High School in Hampton, which was roughly 45 minutes away from her Misty Morning Lane home.

Her interest in heavy metal served Pam well, because it enabled her to forge ties with the programme's often sullen participants. All of the freshmen were obliged to take part. One of these was a lanky, 15-year-old Mötley Crüe fan named Billy Flynn. Seeing Pam for the first time, Flynn is said to have uttered to a friend, 'I'm in love.' Premature, perhaps, but he was smitten. And when, in early February 1990, Pam revealed that she was attracted to him, Flynn's adolescent fantasies came alive.

Their initial encounters did not amount to much. However, in late March, when Greg was obliged to attend an insurance meeting out of state, Pam took the opportunity to further the relationship. She invited Cecelia and Billy to her townhouse, where they drank and watched films. Pam eventually sent her intern out into the cold to walk Halen. She then lured Billy into the bedroom, donned a negligee bought for the occasion and had sex with the high school student. It was Billy's first time.

As their sexual encounters became more frequent, so did Pam's demands that Billy do something about her husband. She told her young lover that Greg beat her, but she could not divorce him for fear of losing the furniture, the wedding gifts and – most of all – Halen. Pam's message to Billy could not have been clearer: 'If you want to keep seeing me, you'll have to get rid of my husband.'

PLANS FOR MURDER

Billy could not face losing Pam so he agreed to kill Greg. Plans were made, but when the moment for murder came the high school student found that he just could not do it. More plans were made and again Billy backed down. Sweet talk was then replaced by anger. 'If you loved me, you'd do this!' Pam screamed at her teenage lover. After hearing those words, Billy knew that he could not fail a third time. Desperate, he turned to his two best friends, Patrick 'Pete' Randall and Vance 'JR' Lattime. Known as the Three Musketeers, they had grown up together and had often earned money by shovelling snow from neighbourhood driveways and walks. With a fourth teenager, Raymond 'Rayme' Fowler, they were now about to embark on a different kind of employment – one that offered a much higher payment.

Pam had promised to give Pete and JR part of the money from Greg's life insurance policy if they would murder Greg. Billy, of course, would get the 'Maiden of Metal' to himself. The plan, as she laid it out, was quite simple. The four boys would drive to a nearby shopping plaza, where JR and Rayme would wait, while Billy and Pete broke into the Misty Morning Lane townhouse. This would not prove too difficult, because Pam would make certain that the cellar and the rear doors were unlocked. Billy and Pete would then ransack the townhouse in order to make it look as if Greg had stumbled upon a burglary. Pam allowed the boys a good deal of latitude at this point – the pair could take whatever they wished.

There were, however, some fairly strict instructions. Halen was to be put in the basement, so that he would not be traumatized by the murder. Pam also insisted that the boys use a gun – not a knife – because she did not want to run the risk of Greg's blood staining her white leather sofa.

RINGS ON HER FINGERS

On 1 May 1990, Pam arrived late for work. She had needed to stay at home until Greg had left the house, so that the doors could be left unlocked. With rings on every finger and a number of gold necklaces hanging around her neck she looked a little odd, but she was playing it safe. She did not want to run the risk of her jewellery being stolen in the faux burglary that was about to take place.

It was a very good day for the murder. An after hours school board meeting ensured that she would not arrive home until long after Greg had been killed. The only glitch came when Billy telephoned to say that he needed a lift to pick up the getaway car – an old Chevrolet that belonged to JR's grandmother.

At about 8.30pm Greg arrived home. The young insurance salesman had barely entered the townhouse when he was overpowered by Billy and Pete. He gave the intruders his wallet, but when Pete demanded his wedding ring, Greg refused. He said, 'No. I can't do that. My wife would kill me.' They were to be Greg Smart's final words. Billy stepped forward. After asking God's forgiveness he then shot Greg in the head. The fake burglars sprinted out of the back of the townhouse. They were running towards JR, Rayme and the getaway car. As they drove away they passed Pam, who flicked her headlights in greeting.

SUSPICIOUS BEHAVIOUR

This carefree and careless attitude was typical of the behaviour that would bring Pam Smart down. Several members of the Derry Police Department could not help but notice that she referred to her husband as 'the body' and that her greatest concern was for Halen. Three days after the murder, the police took Pam back to the crime scene so that she could pick up some personal items. They watched with interest as the widow walked back and forth over a patch of bloodstained carpet.

Fourteen days into the investigation, the Derry police had the first of several lucky breaks when they received a call from an anonymous female. She told them that Pam's assistant Cecelia Pierce knew all about the murder. Then on 14 June Cecelia broke down and told the Derry Police all she knew. Only six weeks had passed since Billy had killed Greg and yet Pam's carefully laid plans had already crumbled. Only days earlier, JR's father had walked into Seabrook's police station with his snub-nosed .38 calibre revolver, thinking that it might have been used in the murder. Worse still, Pete and JR had been overheard discussing the crime, a slip that had resulted in the arrest of the four boys.

Though Pam was becoming suspicious, she spoke openly to Cecelia in four conversations that were recorded by the police. She was bold to the end, declaring that no one would ever believe the word of someone like JR over her own. 'Me, with a professional reputation, and of course that I teach. You know, that's the thing. They are going to believe me.' In fact, it was JR who would be believed. On 1 August, Pam was arrested at her school board office and seven months later she went on trial, charged with first degree murder.

Speaking to the court, Pam acknowledged her affair

with Billy. She had wanted to keep the sexual relationship hidden from the investigation, she said, because she feared losing her professional standing. The widow speculated that Billy had committed the murder because she had wanted to work things out with her late husband. Then she tried to explain away the taped conversations with Cecelia by telling the court that they were part of an attempt to do some investigating of her own.

The jury would have none of it. On 22 March 1991, after just over 13 hours of deliberation, they returned to court with a guilty verdict. Pamela Smart was sentenced to life imprisonment without the possibility of parole.

Having turned state's evidence, Billy Flynn and Pete Randall got off more lightly. They each received 40 year sentences for the murder. Their friends, JR Lattime and Rayme Fowler, were sentenced to 30 years' imprisonment. In subsequent hearings, Pam would be found guilty of two more crimes: conspiracy to commit first degree murder and tampering with a witness.

After the first conviction, Derry police captain Loring Jackson, spoke about Pam Smart. 'She thought she was smart, but she had no street smarts. Nine-year-olds have more street smarts than she had. That was the problem. She thought she was smarter than the whole world. But she made many mistakes, right and left.'

SUSAN SMITH
making a play for
the boss's son

The evening of 25 October 1994 was very mild and pleasant, a nice night for a drive. Susan Smith was doing just that. With her two sons sleeping in the back seat, she drove her 1990 Mazda Protégé along Highway 49 to John D Long Lake. It was not a place she had ever visited before. She parked in the middle of the boat launch, got out and released the brake. The car carrying her sons entered the lake. They were strapped in the back seat. It floated at first, then it slowly took in water before submerging.

Minutes later, Susan was at a local house pleading for help. The story she told had no basis in truth, yet for a time it held the hearts of a nation. There was a wave of sympathy for this poor young mother who had lost her two children.

Susan Leigh Vaughan, later Susan Smith, was born on 26 September 1971. She was raised in Union, South Carolina, a bleak industrial city with a per capita income of $9,230. Susan's childhood was made difficult by the circumstances of her parents' marriage. Linda, Susan's mother, was pregnant with another man's child when she married Harry, Susan's father. The boy was named Michael. Harry and Linda also had a son between them, whom they called Scotty. And then, of course, there was Susan.

After such a start to the marriage, Harry could never really get over the idea that his wife was being unfaithful. He drank heavily and argued incessantly with Linda. At times he threatened to kill her and then himself. Then Michael – Susan's half-brother – had to be treated at Duke University Medical Center after he tried to kill himself.

The divorce of Susan's parents, in 1977, brought no peace. Harry's alcoholism became more serious. On one occasion he broke into his ex-wife's house and assaulted her. He then asked the attending police officers to arrest him before he could do any more harm.

Not long afterwards, Susan's father placed a rifle between his legs and shot himself in the stomach. It was a messy suicide attempt. Harry did not die immediately. Instead he suffered unimaginable pain as he called for help and was taken to the hospital. Though he underwent emergency surgery, Susan's father could not be saved.

Linda had quickly moved on. Within two weeks of her divorce from Harry she had married Beverly (Bev) Russell, a successful businessman who served on the executive of the South Carolina State Republican Party. He was also a member of the advisory board of the Christian Coalition. With a new stepfather came a new home. Susan and Scotty moved with their mother into Bev's spacious home in Union's Mount Vernon Estates section. It was there, shortly before her 16th birthday in 1987, that Susan was first molested by her stepfather. The acts continued for some time, eventually resulting in a legal agreement that remains sealed to the public.

SEXUAL RELATIONS

In the summer of 1988 Susan got a job at Winn-Dixie,

a local supermarket. Susan soon began having sexual relations with two of her co-workers, one of whom was a married man. She became pregnant by the married man and had an abortion. At this point the married boyfriend found out about the other relationship, so he ended his association with Susan. Distraught, the 17-year-old attempted suicide with the aid of Tylenol and aspirin. After some time off, Susan returned to work and began a new relationship with yet another Winn-Dixie co-worker, David Smith.

The two had something in common in that they had both experienced very unhealthy family lives. David's father, a Vietnam veteran who worked at Wal-Mart, was in constant conflict with his mother over her devotion as a Jehovah's Witness. David took his father's side. Dismissing his mother's faith, he lived with his brother at the home of their paternal grandmother.

David was not exactly a free man when he began his relationship with Susan. Although he was just 19 years old, he was engaged to another girl. He concealed the relationship from his fiancée until January 1991, when

Susan announced that she was pregnant with his child. With the news out in the open, the engagement was off. Released from his obligation, David was free to marry Susan Vaughan. On 15 March 1991, the couple got married in nearby Bogansville. After the wedding, Susan joined David in his grandmother's house. She had lived there for just two weeks when her new father-in-law attempted suicide. The incident finally brought the marriage of David's parents to an end.

On 10 October 1991, Susan gave birth to a son they named Michael Daniel Smith. It was a joyous occasion in what was already a very rocky marriage. The couple had serious differences when it came to money – David felt that Susan was spending beyond their means. And then they both began having extramarital affairs. These relationships led to a number of brief separations. In November 1992, Susan again became pregnant, apparently by David. The couple were encouraged to purchase their first home, an act that was meant to provide some sort of stability, but the plan failed. In June 1993 David took up with another of his supermarket colleagues. Two months later, a second son, Alexander Tyler Smith, was born.

BAD SITUATION

The children and the house had not made the marriage any more stable. In August of 1993, the same month that baby Alex was born, David moved out of their new home.

By this point, Susan no longer wanted to work at Winn-Dixie. The couple's affairs with their co-workers had been a bad enough problem, but even worse was the fact that David was Susan's supervisor. Susan got a job at Conso Products, a manufacturer of decorative items, the largest employer in Union. She enjoyed the work and she also enjoyed the attention she received from the owner's son, 27-year-old Tom Findlay. He was not what one could call a handsome man – his features were rather ordinary and he was losing his hair. However, as the son of one of Union's wealthiest men, Tom was considered a real catch.

In the summer of 1994, Susan and David made one last half-hearted attempt to save their marriage and then they agreed to go their separate ways. Susan was happy to return to dating Tom. In September, she had David served with divorce papers. All seemed to be going well for Susan. An unsatisfactory marriage had ended and she was looking forward to a life with a new man. Then came a bombshell. On 17 October 1994, Tom sat down at a computer and composed a letter to Susan. His message was quite blunt.

Susan, I could really fall for you. You have some endearing qualities about you, and I think that you are a terrific person. But like I have told you before, there are some things about you that aren't suited for me, and yes, I am speaking about your children.

However, Tom's rejection of Susan – because that is what it was – was not just about his reluctance to raise children that had been fathered by another man. He wrote of a recent hot tub party he had held at which a naked Susan had kissed and fondled a friend's husband.

· 'If you want to catch a nice guy like me one day,' he wrote, 'you have to act like a nice girl. And you know, nice girls don't sleep with married men.'

PROMISCUOUS

Susan found the letter hard to swallow so she confronted Tom at his cottage. She sought to garner sympathy by telling him about her relationship with her stepfather, but this revelation only served to shock the man she wanted to marry. Although she had set her cap at Tom, Susan juggled a number of sexual relationships during the autumn of 1994. Her behaviour was becoming increasingly erratic. On 25 October 1994, hours before murdering her two children, Susan asked to leave work early – yet she remained at her desk. She told her supervisor that she was in love with Tom, but he didn't love her. Then she added a chilling statement: 'It can never be... because of my children.'

Things became even more bizarre when Susan asked Tom to come to her office. She told him a fanciful story about some embarrassing information that David had threatened to make public during the forthcoming divorce proceedings. David was going to tell the court that she had been having an affair with Tom's father. What was more, she went on, the allegation was true. Then in the middle of the afternoon Susan tried to return

Tom's university sweatshirt, without success. She later went to his office in order to apologize for lying about the affair with his father. By this point, Tom could take no more, so he escorted her from the room.

Just a few hours later, Susan let her sons drown in John D Long Lake.

The first person to have any idea that something was amiss was Shirley McCloud. She had just finished reading the local newspaper when Susan appeared on her front porch. She was crying. According to Shirley, Susan had said: 'A black man has got my kids and my car.' Susan's story soon became more elaborate. When she had stopped at a red light an armed black man had leapt into her car. After threatening to kill her, he had made her drive for several miles before making her get out. At this point she was not far from Shirley's house. He would not let Susan retrieve her children from the back seat. All he said was, 'I don't have time.'

Susan's story, while very dramatic, was highly suspicious. Yet many took it to be true. A great number of people were called upon to help in the search for Susan's missing children. Divers even combed the bottom of John D Long Lake, but they concentrated on the wrong area. Working with the distressed mother, a sketch artist produced a composite drawing that depicted a middle-aged black man with dark knit cap, dark shirt, blue jeans and a plaid jacket. Then with Susan by his side, David made a televised appeal to the carjacker:

> To whoever has our boys, we ask that you please don't hurt them and bring them back. We love them very much. I plead to the guy please return our children to us safe and unharmed. Everywhere I look, I see their play toys and pictures. They are both wonderful children. I don't know how else to put it. And I can't imagine life without them.

AREAS OF DOUBT

Exactly when the authorities began to suspect Susan is not known. After all, no one wants to admit that they were taken in by her story. What is certain is that on 27 October, two days after the supposed abductions, Susan was given the first of several polygraph tests. The results contained areas of doubt. Her interviews with the police also revealed a number of inconsistencies. What is more, Susan claimed to have visited Wal-Mart with her children, but not one person working in the store could recall the event. Within a few days of Susan's tearful appearance on the McClouds' front porch, the attention of the authorities was firmly fixed upon her.

On the morning of 3 November, the ninth day of the children's disappearance, Susan appeared with David on a number of nationally broadcast shows. She appealed for the return of her sons. 'Whoever did this is a sick and emotionally unstable person,' she said. The sorry charade came to an end that afternoon. Confronted with the overwhelming amount of contradictory evidence she had provided, Susan confessed to killing her sons.

Susan Smith's trial began on 19 July 1995. The prosecution argued that Susan had sacrificed her children in the hope of a rosy future with the son of a wealthy industrialist, while the defence focused on the abuse she had suffered at the hands of her stepfather. It was submitted that she had lived a hard life and that she had sought to end it by perishing with her sons in John D Long Lake. However, at the last possible moment she had left the car, allowing Michael and Alex to die alone.

On 22 July, after a three day trial, a jury found Susan guilty of two counts of murder. Despite the best efforts of the prosecution, she was spared the death penalty. Instead, she was sentenced to 30 years' imprisonment. Susan Smith will be eligible for parole in 2025.

LYNN TURNER
murder by
antifreeze

Glenn Turner and Randy Thompson had a great deal in common. They had both worked as police officers in their respective communities and they had both been in love with the same woman, an attractive brunette who called herself Lynn. Both men also died less than a day after visiting a hospital emergency room, even though they had been seemingly healthy men in their early thirties. The cause of death in both cases had been an irregular heartbeat.

Julia 'Lynn' Womak was working as a 911 dispatcher when she first met Glenn Turner, a police officer in Cobb County, Georgia. Theirs was a fun courtship.

Lynn spoiled her boyfriend terribly with expensive gifts. They included snakeskin boots with a matching belt and tickets to see the Atlanta Braves play in the World Series. On 21 August 1993, Lynn and Glenn were married at Johnson Ferry Baptist Church, 20 miles (30 kilometres) outside Atlanta. Their union was not a happy one. Within a few months, Lynn's spending was straining the marriage. Two Chevrolet Camaros alone cost $50,000. Glenn was forced to take a second job at a gas station.

It was not just the money. Six months after the couple had exchanged vows they were sleeping in separate beds. Lynn told her husband that she was having 'female problems', but a more likely reason for the change in sleeping arrangements was that she was being satisfied elsewhere. Lynn had begun having an affair with Randy Thompson. What Glenn knew of the affair is uncertain. However, a friend would later testify in court that the police officer-cum-gas station attendant was tortured by the relationship.

In February of 1995, while Lynn was reportedly in Daytona with Randy, Glenn confided in a friend. 'When she gets home tonight, we're going to work it out. I want to work my marriage out. I love her, but I can only take so much.'

Glenn might have wanted to work things out with his wife, but he was running out of time. And it appeared that Lynn was not that interested. On 20 February 1995, about a year into his wife's affair with Randy, Glenn told a fellow police officer that Lynn had threatened to shoot him with his service revolver. Ten days after that, on 2 March, Glenn entered the Kennestone Hospital emergency room complaining of a severe headache, nausea, vomiting, diarrhoea and nosebleeds. He was given fluids intravenously for his dehydration, after which he felt significantly better. A little over four hours later he was released. On the following day, Lynn walked into the bedroom she shared with her husband and found him dead. The autopsy report recorded that an irregular heartbeat had been the cause of death.

Glenn was buried on 6 March. Lynn was in a state of great irritation and aggravation when she attended her late husband's funeral. The police department wanted to drape Glenn's casket with the Stars and Stripes, but Lynn was totally against the idea. She is quoted as saying some strange things.

Aw, dammit, who the f*** does the Cobb County Police Department think they are? I am in charge of this f***ing funeral. I don't want no f***ing flag on there. If they keep messing with me I'll shut this f***ing thing down.

Four days later, Lynn submitted an apartment rental application in which she listed Randy as the co-occupant. Glenn's death allowed Lynn to pursue her relationship with Randy without hindrance. Three months after the death, they went on a cruise with another couple. Lynn footed the bill, something she could well afford after having collected roughly $153,000 on Glenn's various insurance policies. She also received a widow's pension amounting to $788 each month.

Lynn and Randy lived together for roughly four years. Though the couple did not marry, they did have two children together. It was a turbulent relationship.

In 1996, Lynn appeared at a hospital emergency room saying that Randy had pushed her in a drunken rage. The next year, he took an overdose of pain killers and sleeping pills. Randy also pleaded guilty to assault and battery against Lynn, for which he was sentenced to ten months probation. Although they were told to stay apart, the pair continued to live together until the autumn of 1999. Despite the break-up, though, they continued seeing one another.

OVER THE LIMITS

On her own for the first time since her marriage to Glenn, 6 years earlier, Lynn began to fall into debt. By 2001, she was regularly pushing her credit cards over their limits and she had overdrawn her bank account on more than 30 occasions. Each infringement had been accompanied by a penalty. In early January of that year, Lynn informed a bank representative that she would soon be able to tackle her unpaid fees. On 19 January 2001, the estranged couple and their children had dinner together at a local steakhouse and then went back to Lynn's house for dessert. Early the next morning, Randy went to a hospital emergency room with flu-like symptoms. As he had been vomiting, he was given fluids and an anti-vomiting medication. He was then released, after which he returned to his apartment – but he died alone less than 24 hours later. An autopsy concluded that he had died of heart disease.

Lynn received roughly $36,000 on Randy's life insurance. There would have been so much more, but Randy had let a $400,000 life insurance policy lapse some 11 days before he died. Three weeks after Randy's death, the late fireman's mother received a most unusual piece of correspondence. The letter was from Kathy Turner, the mother of Glenn Turner. After hearing the news of Randy's death she had noticed that his symptoms had been strikingly similar to those of her own son. Due to the efforts of the two women, a Georgia Bureau of Investigation forensic pathologist tested tissue samples taken from Randy's body. He discovered calcium oxalate crystals – a constituent of antifreeze. On 30 July 2002, Glenn Turner's body was also exhumed. It had been six years in the ground, but the tell-tale crystals could still be detected.

As it turned out, Glenn and Randy are the only known victims of antifreeze poisoning in the State of Georgia.

Both men would have suffered horribly. The early symptoms of antifreeze poisoning are much the same as might be experienced after a few glasses of wine: slurred speech, combined with a slight dizziness. But 24 hours later, things become very unpleasant indeed. First there is a horrible headache, followed by increasing dizziness, nausea and hyperventilation. The body then tries to rid itself of the poison through vomiting and diarrhoea. This additional suffering is all to no avail. What is required is an antidote, without which the victim will almost certainly die.

On 1 November 2002, Lynn Turner was indicted for the murder of Glenn Turner. Despite objections, the prosecution was allowed to present the autopsy reports made after Randy's death. Lynn's defence counsel tried to show the court that the police evidence was invalid. They also advanced the argument that Randy could have committed suicide. After all, he had made a suicide attempt in 1997. But their efforts would not sway the jury.

On the afternoon of 14 May 2004, Lynn entered the courtroom to hear the jury's verdict. It had been a long trial. Lynn said she was ready for any conclusion – she would, she claimed, display no emotion. Sure enough, when the jury foreman rose to announce that she had been found guilty of the death of her husband, Glenn Turner, Lynn remained stone-faced. She was sentenced to life imprisonment, with the possibility of parole after 14 years.

On 8 January 2007, Lynn returned to court – this time to face the charge that she murdered Randy Thompson. After a trial lasting more than two months, she was found guilty of capital murder. Although the prosecution had sought the death penalty, Lynn received a second life sentence for the murder, with no chance of parole.

ROSEMARY WEST
a marriage made
in hell

Rosemary West was no murderer when she met her future husband Fred – but he was to change that. She would soon become his willing accomplice. Eventually she would earn the dubious distinction of being Britain's most prolific female serial killer. The activities of this depraved and murderous couple would result in one of the most sensational British murder trials of the 20th century.

Rosemary Letts, later Rosemary West, was born on 29 November 1953 in the ancient Devon town of Barnstaple. It was the very same place that had produced the poet and dramatist John Gay several centuries earlier. The future murderer was an unaccomplished, unhappy child. Her father, Bill, was a violent schizophrenic who beat his wife and four children and her mother, Daisy, also had mental problems. She suffered from recurring bouts of depression that were so extreme that she had received electric shock treatment. A number of these sessions had taken place while she was pregnant with Rosemary.

It is not surprising, therefore, that Rosemary performed badly at school. Even though many people knew her as Rose, those of her classmates with a penchant for teasing would refer to her as 'Dozy Rosie'. The nickname was an accurate description of a girl who lacked intelligence and was prone to daydreaming. For Rose, adolescence marked the beginning of a losing struggle with her weight. As a result, boys paid little attention to her. But this did not bother her too much because she was more interested in older men.

This predilection for more mature partners would lead her to embark upon a fatal relationship. On her fifteenth birthday, 29 November 1968, she met 27-year-old Fred West.

Several weeks after this meeting, Rose's parents split up. For a time, she lived with an elder sister and her husband. Away from her father's Victorian standards of discipline, she was finally free to venture out in the evenings. And yet, after a few months, Rose returned to her father's home. It was a curious move, one that has led to speculation that the father and his daughter might have shared an incestuous relationship. It was while she was living under her father's watchful eye and threatening hand that Rose's relationship with Fred West became more serious. Bill Letts did not approve of his daughter's new boyfriend, but then few fathers would. After all, Fred, a married man with two children, was a full 12 years older than Rose. Moreover, he had a criminal record. He had twice been fined for theft and at the age of 20 he had been found guilty of having sex with a 13-year-old girl. Not only that, he had accidentally run over and killed a young boy while he had been driving an ice cream van.

FRED'S PAST

What, if anything, Bill Letts knew of this sorry story is unknown. However, it is certain that he knew nothing about Fred's connection with the death of a young woman named Anna McFall.

In 1967 the 18-year-old Anna became pregnant by Fred. It is possible that she had done so intentionally as a means of pressuring Fred to divorce Rena, his wife of five years. If so, her plan went tragically wrong. Instead of giving in to Anna's demands, Fred killed her. Then in July 1967 he buried her pregnant body near the trailer park in which they had lived. If the records are correct, this horrific event was Fred's first murder. It would be followed by another killing only six months later, when he abducted Mary Bastholm, a 15-year-old waitress, from a Gloucester bus stop.

Even though he was entirely unaware that his daughter was dating a murderer, Bill Letts still complained to the relevant social services department. Then he threatened Fred by showing up at his home. Both of these actions were ineffective, but then things changed of their own accord. Fred was soon forced to put his relationship with Rose on hold after he was convicted of a number of thefts. A brief stint in prison followed, during which time Rose discovered that she was pregnant. Without more ado she moved out of her father's house and into

Fred's home on Midland Road in Gloucester.

Now she was living with her boyfriend for the first time, Rose found the accommodation was not to her liking. The house was cramped and she was obliged to look after Charmaine and Anna Marie, the two daughters Fred had fathered by his wife, Rena. The living space became tighter still when, on 17 October 1970, Rose gave birth to a baby girl she named Heather.

Two months later, Fred was once again convicted of theft. He spent more than six months in prison, during which time Charmaine disappeared. Rose told Anna Marie that Fred's wife Rena had taken her sister away. In actual fact, Rose had murdered the girl not long after her eighth birthday. After his release from prison, Fred removed Charmaine's fingers, toes and kneecaps and then he buried what remained of her corpse beneath the kitchen floor.

RENA'S FATE

The girl might have been out of sight, but she was not out of mind. Some time later, Rena called round to ask about her daughter. For Fred, the solution to this rather threatening situation was obvious. In August 1971, less than two months after his release from prison, he killed his wife and buried her not far from where the corpse of Anna McFall lay hidden. Fred and Rose then fell into a pattern of entertaining all and sundry, which gave them quite a reputation within Gloucester's West Indian community. A great many men visited the Midland Road address. Some paid money to have sex with Rose, while others enjoyed the privilege for no payment. Fred would often watch through a peephole. Personal advertisements featuring Rose were then placed in 'swinger magazines'.

In the autumn of 1971, Rose again became pregnant, apparently with Fred's child. The couple married a few months later at the Gloucester Registry Office. When the baby they named Mae West was born, she could quite rightly be described as legitimate. Not long afterwards, the family – or what was left of it – packed up and moved to 25 Cromwell Street. A much larger place than their last home, it included a cellar in which Fred had installed soundproofing. It was going to be used as a 'torture chamber', he said. The description was apt. Within a few months, he and Rose led Anna Marie, then eight years old, down the cellar steps. They told her how lucky she was to have such considerate parents and then they undressed her. She was informed that her father would show her how to satisfy a future husband. The girl was then raped as Rose pinned her down. This horrific experience marked the beginning of an eight-year ordeal that would only end when Anna Marie became old enough to escape the house.

By the closing months of 1972, the Wests' day-to-day existence consisted of violence, theft, rape, incest, torture, prostitution, voyeurism, pornography and paedophilia. Into this mix they introduced an attractive 17-year-old girl, Caroline Owens, hired as the family's nanny. Fred and Rose assured the girl's parents that they would watch over their daughter.

Caroline did receive a great deal of attention from the Wests, but it was not what she had been led to expect. She attempted to leave after Fred and Rose had failed to seduce her, but the couple prevented her from escaping.

After being taken to the 'torture chamber', the girl was stripped naked and raped. Seeking to keep Caroline under his control, Fred issued a chilling threat.

'I'll keep you in the cellar and let my black friends have you, and when we're finished we'll kill you and bury you under the paving stones of Gloucester.'

HORRIBLE BRUISES

Fred's intimidating behaviour worked for a time. But then Caroline's mother noticed the horrible bruises on her daughter's body and called the police. In January 1973, Fred and a pregnant Rose appeared before a magistrate to answer charges stemming from the numerous assaults on their nanny. But Caroline could not go through the ordeal of providing evidence, so the couple escaped prison. They walked away after paying £100 in fines for indecent assault.

Now lacking a nanny, Fred and Rose welcomed a 21-year-old seamstress named Lynda Gough to the Cromwell Street address. The Wests seem to have taken violent exception to Lynda. She was killed and buried in the back garden. When her family inquired after her, Fred and Rose said that she had simply decided to leave.

In August 1973, Rose gave birth to the couple's first son, a healthy baby named Stephen. Three months later, at about the time of Rose's twentieth birthday, she and Fred abducted, sexually abused and strangled a 15-year-old student named Carol Ann Cooper. Two days after Christmas, the couple murdered their third victim of the year, a promising university student named Lucy Partington. Over the next four years, four more females, aged 15 to 21, would become trapped in Fred and Rose's Cromwell Street home. All of them would be sexually abused, tortured, killed and buried somewhere on the property.

The Wests' gruesome routine was disrupted somewhat in 1977. Fred remodelled the house in order to take in lodgers. One of the first of these guests was an 18-year-old prostitute named Shirley Robinson, with whom both Fred and Rose enjoyed sexual relations. Both women became pregnant within months of each other. While Shirley carried her landlord's child, Rose had been made pregnant by one of her West Indian clients.

THREAT TO THE MARRIAGE?

Relations between the two women soured over the course of their pregnancies. Rose came to view Shirley as a threat to her marriage. She felt that the younger prostitute was plotting to take her place. And so, not long after giving birth, Rose made certain that her rival and the unborn baby joined the other women and girls beneath the Wests' home.

While torture and sexual abuse remained the norm, the 1979 murder of Alison Chambers, a 17-year-old runaway, would mark something of a break in the chain of death. In the previous eight years, together or apart, Fred and Rose had murdered a total of eleven girls and women. In the meantime, Rosemary continued to prove herself extremely fertile. By 1983, she had given birth to eight children – five by Fred and three by her West Indian clients.

When Anna Marie left the house to live with a boyfriend, it created an abyss in Fred's sex life that was filled by two other daughters, Heather and Mae. Heather was the eldest of Fred and Rose's children and it was she who betrayed them. In 1987, she told a friend that she had been physically and sexually abused by her father. She went on to say that her mother had been sleeping with other men. When these claims got back to her parents, Heather was killed. The remaining children were told that their sister run away from home, when in reality she was buried in the back garden.

Fred had enjoyed an incredible string of good luck for a complete decade. Rapes and murders aside, he had continued with his criminal activities. The police had every excuse to visit his house on Cromwell Street, with its torture chamber, but it looked as if he would never be caught.

However, in the summer of 1992 Fred West's luck would finally turn. A girl that he had raped with Rose's help told a friend about her experience. The friend then went to the police. On 6 August 1992 the authorities turned up at the house with a search warrant. When the police left they took the Wests with them, in handcuffs. Fred was charged with the rape and sodomy of a minor, while Rose was accused of assisting in the assault. But as the police soon discovered, there was much more to unravel than an assault charge. Anna Marie told the police the story of how she had been abused, which was shocking enough. But then she went on to talk about the mysterious disappearances of Charmaine and Heather.

SMOKE SCREEN

A further 18 months passed before Rose answered the door of her Cromwell Street home on the afternoon of 24 February 1994 to find the police on the doorstep. They were ready to dig up the back garden. Fred soon showed up, but not before he had stopped off at the police station. His aim was to create a smoke screen by telling the authorities that Heather had been a troubled child: a lesbian who had a drug problem.

On the very next morning he confessed that he had indeed killed his daughter. He even went so far as to provide a detailed description of how he had cut up her body. However, he went back on his story 15 minutes later. This time he told the police that Heather had worked for a drug cartel in Bahrain, under an alias. When the excavation turned up human bones, Fred changed his story yet again. He admitted that he had killed Heather, but he said that it had been an accident. As more bodies turned up, more confessions were made. In all of this time, though, Fred maintained that the murders had been nothing whatsoever to do with Rose.

VICTIM OF A MADMAN

Rose was not nearly so faithful a spouse. She turned on Fred in an attempt to portray herself as the victim of a madman. It was not a convincing performance, nor was it supported by the evidence. Still, she kept up the pretence to the end.

At their joint hearing, she rejected her husband's attempts to console her. She told the police that he made her sick. On New Year's Day 1995, Fred hanged himself in his cell at Birmingham's Winson Green Prison.

Rose was tried ten months later. Anna Marie, Caroline Owens and another woman gave testimony concerning her sexual assaults on them. Rose's defence team were willing to concede that Rose might have committed sexual assault. However, they contended that she had been entirely unaware that her late husband was killing girls and young women.

Defiant, belligerent and angry, the accused came off very badly on the stand. But the greatest blow to the defence came from a woman named Janet Leach. Fred had earlier told her about an understanding that he had entered into with Rose. He had agreed to take all of the blame for the killings when the time came – including the murders of Charmaine and Shirley Robinson, which had been committed by Rose alone.

Rose was ultimately found guilty of ten murders and was sentenced to life imprisonment. In her case, the sentence means what it says. She is the only woman serving a sentence in a British prison who does not have the option of release or parole.

LISA WHEDBEE
church
love triangle

It was in a house of worship – Trinity United Methodist Church in Knoxville, Tennessee, to be precise – that romance bloomed. To those who knew nothing of their backgrounds, they would have looked like a pleasant, well-matched couple. Lisa Whedbee's lovely voice was an asset to the choir and Michael Frazier was the popular organist and choir director. However, the pair took great pains to hide their relationship. Adultery was something their church frowned upon.

Lisa was born Lisa Carol Outlaw in the suburbs of Knoxville. Beautiful, blond and athletic, she was the sort of girl who turned heads. And in 1979, she did just that. Riding around with her friends one night, she pulled up alongside a Corvette. The car belonged to 19-year-old Rob Whedbee. The two began dating and they were married two years later, shortly after Lisa graduated from high school. In 1986, the couple were joined by a son, whom they named Justin. Four years later, they had another child, Brittany, a daughter born with Down's Syndrome.

According to Rob, the news of their newborn daughter's condition had changed Lisa. Though neither he nor Lisa had been what you might call churchgoers, his wife became a regular at Trinity United Methodist Church. By 1993, her involvement had extended to the church choir, under the guidance of choir director Michael Frazier. The son of a pastor, Michael was a journalist with the Oak Ridger, a small community newspaper located in the city of Oak Ridge, about half an hour west of Knoxville.

One of Michael's better articles was written for Mother's Day 1993. It dealt with Lisa and her challenges as the mother of a child with Down's Syndrome. Titled 'A Mother's Nightmare, A Mother's Dream', the piece featured a large full-colour photograph of mother and daughter. But while Michael was lavish in his praise of

Lisa's devotion to Brittany, he failed to mention that the mother was not raising the child alone. As a result, Rob's name was entirely absent from the story.

BOMBSHELL

A few weeks after the article was published, Michael and Lisa were standing in the Trinity United Methodist Church car park after choir practice when Lisa suddenly came out with a bombshell. She told Michael that she had feelings for him. Once the truth was out, the relationship moved quickly – by July the couple were meeting for sex. Nine months into the affair, Lisa consulted an attorney regarding divorce. While it was obvious that her affections lay elsewhere, she reported that her marriage had become unhealthy in other ways. Then on 17 May, Lisa filed a petition for a protection order. She alleged that Rob had been enraged by her meeting with the divorce lawyer. In the court document, Lisa painted a picture of Bob that many would not recognize.

'He told me that my attorney would not ever make it to court for me because he would kill her first, then he would kill my best friend for helping me.'

There was one bright spot in the midst of all this acrimony – Michael had won a Tennessee Associated Press Managing Editors Association award for his feature on Lisa and Brittany. The presentation was scheduled for 24 June. But as it would turn out, Michael would be otherwise engaged. Shortly after supper time on 7 June 1994, Lisa picked Michael up at his apartment and drove him to her house. Armed with a butcher's knife, he hid in a downstairs closet, waiting for the right moment. The couple planned to murder Rob.

HIDING PLACE

After Rob finished work that night he did not come directly home. Instead he played softball with friends. When he finally got home he had something to eat and then he started to attend to some paperwork. At that point, Lisa walked into the room wearing a negligee. She led him upstairs to bed, where they had sex. At about two o'clock in the morning, when her husband seemed to be in a deep sleep, Lisa went to Michael's hiding place. The choirmaster pulled a stocking over his face, donned rubber gloves and followed Lisa to the master bedroom. But when he looked down on the sleeping man, he found that he could not do it – he was no murderer.

If only Michael had been a little more careful it might have ended there, with Rob none the wiser. However, when Lisa's lover turned to leave he bumped into the corner of the marital bed. Rob was startled awake. A terrified Michael then began stabbing at Rob, cutting his hand and arm in several places. Rob managed to pin his assailant against the wall. He was a weight lifter and a former boxer, after all. When she heard the two men struggling, Lisa came into the room holding an aluminium baseball bat. At first, her husband thought rescue was at hand, so he called to his wife to turn on the light. But she did not move. He then asked her to call the police, but again she remained motionless. At first he was dumbfounded and then he noticed that she was creeping ever so slowly closer. Then he heard his attacker yell, 'You've gotta do it – and you've gotta do it now!'

BETRAYED

Rob immediately recognized his attacker's voice. He also

realized that he had been betrayed. Worst of all, though, he was outnumbered. He picked the choir director up and tossed him against a night table – then he grabbed for the bat and ran from the room. The attacker dashed behind him in hot pursuit. They ran through the darkened house until Rob reached the garage. There under the harsh shadeless light, with the bat in his hand, he turned to confront his attacker. Michael was a much smaller man, so he quickly backed down and fled the garage, locking the door behind him. The wronged husband began beating on the door, trying to get in. This awoke a neighbour, who called the police. Although the sheriff's deputies took only minutes to arrive, Michael was nowhere to be found. He had run from the house and into the neighbouring woods.

Lisa immediately put on an act. She pretended to be entirely mystified by the dramatic events that had just taken place within her home. However, she was confronted by her husband. 'She was trying to play, you know, "I don't know what happened... what was going on." She acted like she didn't even know who that was.

And I just basically told her, "That's a bunch of crap."'

Rob told the police that his wife had spoken to his attacker. It was clear to him that she was in on the whole thing. Lisa was arrested and the police then turned their attention to finding the choir director. Michael knew he could not return to his apartment, so he took a long walk to his estranged wife's townhouse. He was arrested there at six o'clock in the morning. A few hours later, Rob filed for divorce.

On 13 September 1995, the choirmaster became the first of the two failed murderers to be tried. The defence did not deny that Michael had planned to kill Lisa's husband, but instead they repeated the allegations that Lisa had made in her petition for an order of protection: 'That he beat her. That he threatened to kill her lawyer. He threatened to kill her best friend.' These, he argued, were legitimate reasons for desperate actions.

When Rob took the witness stand he totally denied that he had ever beat his wife. He went on to say that Lisa's claims about his threats were nothing more than lies. In fact, Rob had stated in a preliminary hearing that it was not he but his wife who had been the abusive one in the relationship. He recalled one heated argument that had ended with Lisa pointing a loaded shotgun in his direction.

NO CHOICE

Nevertheless, Lisa's allegation had been made to the jury. In Michael's view, the defence argued, he had no choice but to help his lover escape years of abuse.

'I was going to do whatever I had to do to protect Lisa,' the choirmaster said on the stand. This testimony, coming from a small, delicate and sensitive man, appeared to have had an effect on the jury. On 16 September, after a trial lasting only three days, Michael was found guilty of the lesser charge of attempted manslaughter. He was sentenced to a prison term of four years.

Nine months after her lover had been convicted, Lisa was brought before a judge. There would be no trial because Lisa had accepted a plea bargain. She did not admit guilt – instead she entered an Alford plea, which is unique to the United States. According to this type of plea the defendant does not admit the charge but recognizes that sufficient evidence exists to convince a judge or a jury to find them guilty.

In the end, Lisa received a sentence of less than a year, which was served at Knox County Penal Farm. She has since remarried... but Michael Frazier is not her new husband.

MARY CAROL WINKLER

murder in
the parsonage

Matthew Winkler was the son of a preacher, the grandson of a preacher and the great-grandson of a preacher, so he was destined for the pulpit. His large athletic frame had made him something of a sports star in Decatur, Alabama, the small town in which he had spent much of his youth. Not only that, his warm personality and dazzling smile endeared him to many of those around him.

As a young man, Matthew attended Freed-Hardeman University on the outskirts of Henderson, Tennessee, a very small city some 62 miles (100 kilometres) west of Memphis. It was a natural choice. His father, Pastor Dan

Winkler, was an adjunct professor. A religious university, it was affiliated with the conservative Churches of Christ. As a result, it had very strict guidelines governing modesty in dress and relations with the opposite sex. It was in this restrictive environment that Matthew met a petite young brunette named Mary Freeman.

Nearly a year older than Matthew, Mary was born on 10 December 1973 at Knoxville, Tennessee, a city with a population of approximately 180,000. Though the Freemans were not wealthy, they were somewhat better off than the Winklers. Much of the Freemans' efforts centred around Laurel Church of Christ, where Mary's father served as a lay minister. The church had proved greatly supportive when Mary's younger sister Patricia, a child who had been crippled physically and mentally by meningitis, died of a seizure at the age of eight.

Mary's great goal was to be a teacher, just like her mother. In high school she had been a member of the Future Teachers of America, the very same organization that had once counted serial killer Marie Hilley as a member. After graduation, Mary attended David Lipscomb University in Nashville, an institution 'committed to teach truth as revealed in God's word through daily Bible classes and chapel', before transferring to Freed-Hardeman University. It was here that Mary and Matthew, the couple with the Biblical names, became campus sweethearts. They became engaged after four months of dating and on 20 April 1996 they were married at the Freeman family home in Knoxville. The bride's father performed the ceremony.

Though the couple returned to the university, their stay was short. Mary became pregnant and money grew tight. Then in October 1997 Mary gave birth to a daughter, whom she named Patricia, after the sister she had lost as a child. Two years later, a second girl, Mary Alice (known as Allie) was born. Mary put aside her dreams of becoming a teacher and tried her best to support her young family. She took on a number of low-wage retail jobs and for a time she worked in the post office. In the meantime, Matthew pursued a career in the ministry. One of his most satisfying jobs was teaching Bible classes at Boyd Christian School in the small Tennessee town of McMinnville.

CHANGE IN FORTUNE

Although the couple's struggles had by no means ended, it seemed that 2005 might bring a change in fortune. At the beginning of the year, Matthew became the pulpit preacher of Fourth Street Church of Christ in Selmer, a small Tennessee town just 16 miles (25 kilometres) south of Freed-Hardeman.

The couple and their two daughters moved into the parsonage, a modest bungalow on a large plot not far from the church. Within weeks of settling in, they were blessed with a third daughter, who was named Brianna. Added to the good news was Mary's return to school, where she pursued her teaching degree.

Matthew and Mary seemed well suited to the quiet little town. Their first year passed without incident. The family celebrated Brianna's first birthday on 5 March 2006 in the knowledge that Mary was finally about to realize her long-deferred dream to teach children. On 21 March, Mary reported for her first day as a substitute teacher at Selmer Elementary School. All appeared to go smoothly, though Mary's new colleagues did notice that she spent a bit too much time talking on her mobile telephone. That evening, the Winklers ate takeaway pizza and watched the children's film *Chicken Little*, which Matthew had rented from a nearby store. By 8.30, the girls were in bed.

It was then that the family evening took on a different tone. The young couple began to argue about money, as they had done many times before. It was familiar ground, though the terrain had been made much more difficult by Mary's poor judgement.

Although she was the person who was entrusted with the family finances, she had become involved in internet fraud. The preacher's wife had deposited two fake cheques amounting to $17,500 in the family's bank account and had then transferred a portion of the money to a second bank. Both institutions, the First State Bank and the Regions Bank, were in the process of investigating Mary's activities. The telephone calls that the new substitute teacher had received at work had been from the banks in question. Whether Matthew knew it or not, he and his wife were expected to have a meeting with a banker on the following day.

HUSBAND'S COMPLAINTS

According to Mary, her husband's unhappiness with the sensitive situation caused him to air other complaints: his dissatisfaction with the administration of the church, for instance. Eventually, things calmed down to a point at which they were at least able to relax a bit. They began to watch a movie, but Mary fell asleep. Matthew then woke her up and they went to bed and had sexual relations of a kind that Mary would describe as 'ordinary for us'.

Then, at about six o'clock in the morning, Mary said, the baby began to cry and Matthew literally kicked her out of bed. Both parents went to Brianna's crib. Once there, the preacher placed his hands over the baby's nose and mouth to encourage sleep, a method he had used many times before. Mary did not like him doing this, so she took the baby and rocked her. Matthew then went back to bed. Once Brianna had fallen asleep Mary went to make some coffee. But that was not all. Mary said that she then went to tell Matthew to 'stop being so mean'. Then all became a cloud. Somehow she wound up with a 12 gauge shotgun in her hands. It was a gun that Matthew used to hunt turkeys. She had aimed it at her sleeping husband, Mary said, but she had not pulled the trigger. Even so, there had most certainly been a gunshot. It was not, Mary said, as loud as she had expected it would be. Nevertheless, it was efficient. The preacher took 77 pellets, which punctured several organs and broke his spine. As he lay dying, blood bubbling from his mouth, he managed just one word: 'Why?'

Patricia then entered her parents' bedroom, but was quickly ushered out. She had been awoken by what she would describe in court as a 'big boom or something'. The 8-year-old and her sister Allie were told that their father had been hurt, and that they would all have to leave the house. When Patricia expressed concern for her father, Mary said that help was already on its way.

The mother and her three girls left with nothing save a pair of baby socks and the shotgun. Mary drove the family minivan throughout the night to Jackson, Mississippi, 250 miles (400 kilometres) south of Selmer. She rested for a few hours at an inn, before driving another 250 miles (400 kilometres) to Orange Beach on the Gulf of Mexico.

By the time the mother and her daughters had begun playing in the sand, news of Matthew's death was known to all at the Fourth Street Church of Christ. In fact, some members of the church had discovered his body about 15 hours after Mary had pulled the trigger. When Matthew had not appeared for evening prayers, a delegation of elders had gone to the parsonage to check on the young family. What they found was Matthew's dead body sprawled on the bedroom floor. Their immediate concern was for Mary and the children. Had they been abducted?

Five hundred miles (800 kilometres) away, the dead preacher's wife and daughters were enjoying the hospitality offered by the Orange Beach Sleep Inn. Mary would later testify that she knew she would be caught but she wanted to treat her daughters to the beach. 'I just wanted to be with them,' she would later say, 'before they had bad days, have a happy day.'

The preacher's wife had demonstrated some caution, but not much. Mary had avoided using her credit cards, yet she continued to drive around in the family's Sienna minivan. Eventually, she was spotted making an illegal

U-turn and was pulled over by Jason Whitlock, an Orange Beach police officer. After running the Tennessee plates through the system and realizing what he had on his hands, he called for backup. Whitlock approached the vehicle with caution, thinking that he might find a kidnapper. He was surprised to find Mary and her three daughters, seemingly healthy and unharmed. The shotgun that had been used to kill the dead preacher was safely in its case, never to be used again.

Mary was taken to the Orange Beach Police Department headquarters, where her daughters were given food from McDonald's as she began to talk. At first, she denied shooting her husband, but it was not long before her story began to change. It was, she insisted, a blur – she was not certain what had happened exactly. Eventually, Mary admitted that she had shot her husband. All the while, she was protective of Matthew. Looking towards the inevitable trial, she praised him to the police, 'He was a mighty fine person. No matter what in the end, I don't want him smeared.'

To the prosecutors, Mary's statements were viewed as

clear evidence that the murder was premeditated, and she was charged with murder in the first degree.

OBSESSIVE

Faced with the possibility of a lifetime in prison for their client, Mary's defence team launched a public relations campaign. First of all they organized an article, 'She Killed Her Husband. Why?', which was published in the November 2006 issue of Glamour magazine. The story suggested that Matthew had been obsessive about money and had possibly been abusive towards his wife. Mary's support team also appeared on ABC's Good Morning America, where they put forward the notion that Matthew insisted on being in control.

Although the prosecution were not going for the death penalty, they moved forward in the belief that Mary should be found guilty of first-degree murder. In her testimony, Mary spoke of the hours leading up to Matthew's death.

'I was upset at him because he had really been on me lately,' she said, 'criticizing me for things, the way I walk, the way I eat, everything. It was just building up to this point. I was just tired of it. I guess I just got to a point and snapped.'

While it was true, the defence conceded, that Mary had held the gun, she had not intended pulling the trigger. The actual firing of the gun had been an accident. By fleeing the parsonage, Mary had only been following instinct.

But there was much more. The defence put forward an account of the mental, physical and sexual abuse, not to mention the degradation, that their client had been forced to endure. After her arrest at Orange Beach, Mary had denied that Matthew had abused her in any manner at all. Now, under oath in Tennessee, she told an entirely different story.

To begin with, Mary said that her husband had kicked and punched her and had threatened her with the shotgun.

The preacher had also visited pornography sites on the internet, which he used as a prelude to sex. Mary told the court that Matthew asked her to engage in oral and anal sex, acts she considered to be unnatural. Moreover, the preacher had asked her to wear a miniskirt, a wig and platform heels in bed. These last two objects were displayed before the court as Mary sobbed.

'If you look up spousal abuse in the dictionary,' a lawyer for the defence asserted, 'you're going to see Mary Winkler's picture.'

The ploy worked. After a little more than seven hours of deliberation, a jury consisting of ten women and two men found Mary guilty of voluntary manslaughter.

At her sentencing hearing, the convicted woman portrayed herself as a victim. Mary said that she had 'suffered the loss of someone I love', a reference to the man she had killed.

'I think of Matthew every day, and the guilt, and I always miss him and love him.'

The sentence, handed down on 8 June, consisted of a mere 150 days in prison, with a further 60 days to be served in a mental health facility. These 210 days would be followed by three years probation. Since Mary had already spent 143 days in prison awaiting trial, she endured only one more week before being sent off to the psychiatric hospital.

Sixty-seven days after sentencing, Mary Winkler, the convicted murderer of Matthew Winkler, was released. In August 2008, after a lengthy legal battle with the dead preacher's parents, she was granted full custody of her three children.

MISTY WITHERSPOON
killing to
escape debt

'**I**t was difficult to understand what was going on over the telephone** because she was so upset,' said Mooresville police chief John Crone. He was talking about Misty Witherspoon, who had reported that she had accidentally shot her husband, Quinn, in the head. Officers rushed to the scene, together with emergency workers, but there was nothing to be done. Quinn Witherspoon was most certainly dead – on 23 September 2005, his young life had come to an end.

Misty Keller Witherspoon met every definition of a small town girl. Born in 1973, she had lived her entire life in Mooresville, North Carolina. She was a 17-year-old high school student, hanging out in Mooresville's small downtown when she met Quinn. In 1994 the couple married, one year before Quinn earned his degree in criminal justice. He took a job as a police officer in the neighbouring town of Concord, while Wendy worked in one of Mooresville's small factories.

In 1998, the couple were blessed with a daughter. Misty worked for a further four years until their second and third children arrived, in the shape of twins. The young couple had prepared for their enlarged family by purchasing their first house. It could not be considered luxurious by any means, yet it saddled the couple with high mortgage payments. They soon found themselves pinched for cash. Quinn had already benefited from several salary increases with the Concord police, but he still felt the need to work overtime. The young father also began taking extra jobs outside the department.

EXHAUSTED

Misty's contribution was running the house and overseeing the finances. Then in 2003, when her eldest child began primary school, she took a low-paying job as treasurer and custodian at Whitman Park Baptist Church, the family's place of worship. She was still employed there on the afternoon of Quinn's death. It had been a busy day so far. For a start, there had been the forthcoming camping trip with Quinn's parents to organize. After putting the twins to bed for their afternoon rest, Quinn settled down on the living room couch. He was exhausted after working the previous evening. There was just time for a short nap before he had to pick his eldest daughter up from school. But the little girl would never see her father again.

Misty said that she had been carrying Quinn's .40 calibre Beretta service weapon when she had tripped. The gun had fallen to the floor and discharged itself: a bullet had flown up and hit her husband in the back of the head. Misty quickly called 911.

Dispatcher: 'Mooresville 911, where's your emergency?'
Misty: 'I... I... I was bringing my husband his gun and I tripped and fell with it and it shot.'
Dispatcher: 'It shot?'
Misty: 'Yes, and it shot him in the head!'

The Witherspoon family showed no hesitation in supporting the grieving widow. 'At this point, we're standing behind Misty 100 per cent. We love her. We're praying for her. We're asking everyone to pray for her,' said Quinn's sister, Sabrina Barnes. Quinn was buried with full police honours.

NAGGING DOUBTS

Misty's account of the incident had been tragic and plausible. Everyone at the Mooresville Police Department so much wanted to believe her. It seemed inconceivable that the wife of a fellow police officer would intentionally kill her husband. However, by the next morning, her story was coming under question. That afternoon, investigators returned to the Witherspoon bungalow with a request: would Misty be willing to re-enact the tragic chain of events? If she did so, the police were sure that their nagging doubts would be laid to rest.

Misty agreed. The sequence of events had begun with a search for some hand lotion. She showed the investigators how she had been looking through the shelves of a bathroom closet when she had come upon Quinn's service revolver and holster. Misty said she had accidentally knocked the gun to the floor and had then been worried that it might have been damaged as a result. She had decided to tell her husband about it there and then, so gun in hand she had walked to where he was sleeping. At that point she slipped on a children's storybook and lost her balance. The gun fell from her hand, hit the floor and fired itself.

The investigators were not convinced by Misty's story. It seemed that there were simply too many improbabilities: coming across the gun; knocking it off the shelf; and slipping on the book. And then there was the gun itself. It had somehow delivered a single fatal shot when it had fallen to the ground, Misty had said. But there was a problem with the angle of the wound. While Misty claimed that she had fallen in front of her husband, it was clear that the shot had come from behind.

And so the investigation continued. The police began talking to friends and neighbours in their search for a possible motive for what was beginning to look like a murder. They uncovered no evidence of infidelity or domestic abuse – the Witherspoons appeared to be a loving couple. There was, however, one area of the Witherspoons' family life that seemed in turmoil: the household finances. A friend told police of her suspicion that Misty had been stealing from the church. Her activities had been so obvious and transparent that it took no more than a brief meeting with the pastor to uncover the truth. Misty had paid her family's bills with funds drawn from the church chequing account. She had been able to continue like this for more than a year before she had been caught by her trusting church. The matter was being dealt with quietly, without notifying the authorities.

On 5 October 2005, the Mooresville Police Department announced that Misty Witherspoon had been taken into custody. She was then charged with first degree murder. And yet Quinn's family continued to stand by the young widow. They had believed her story that the shooting had been an accident. Bob Witherspoon, Quinn's father, made a public statement.

We want everyone to know that Quinn's family supports
Misty 100 per cent. We have not and will not waver in our
support of her. She maintains that this was an accident
and we fully believe her regardless of what the police may
think. We know her better than anyone else and we know
that this was a tragic accident. Her love for Quinn was deep
and without question, and our love and support of Misty is
without question.

IDENTITY FRAUD

Misty's murder trial did not begin until 26 June 2007.
But before that could happen the accused needed to rid
herself of another legal problem. On 1 May 2007, she
pleaded guilty to 37 counts of embezzlement and three
counts of financial identity fraud relating to credit cards
that she had taken out in the name of the church. And yet
Misty's church, from which she had stolen over $27,000,
stood beside the Witherspoon family in maintaining her
innocence.

However, the Mooresville police took a very different
view of Misty. They were certain that she had killed her

husband in order to collect on his insurance – a sum of roughly $300,000.

Quinn's family and the Witherspoons' church created a challenge for the prosecution. After all, if they did not believe Misty killed Quinn, why should a jury? Faced with this hurdle, the prosecuting attorney focused on the fact that Misty was under significant financial pressure. The family had fallen three months behind in its mortgage payments and thousands of dollars were outstanding in unpaid bills. The day Quinn was shot, Misty had received a letter from the local power company – the Witherspoons were about to be cut off. Misty had chosen to kill her husband, an act that brought about a sudden improvement in the family's desperate financial situation.

The defence argued otherwise. According to her lawyer, the accused had intended to commit suicide. She had taken Quinn's service revolver from the bathroom closet and then walked over to her sleeping husband. In this scenario Misty had not slipped. Instead, she stood above Quinn for several minutes with the gun against her head. At that point the cat had jumped on to the couch, startling the suicidal woman. Misty had dropped the gun, it had struck her knee and then it had shot Quinn in the back of the head. According to the defence, the accused had lied to the police in order to conceal her intention of taking her own life.

On the afternoon of 16 July 2007, after two days of deliberation, the jury returned to the courtroom to deliver its verdict. Misty Witherspoon was guilty of murder in the first degree. She was sentenced to life without parole.

Quinn's family remain convinced of their daughter-in-law's innocence.

SUSAN WRIGHT
stabbing, stabbing and
more stabbing

Jeff Wright was killed in his bedroom. It must have been a bloody scene at the time. After all, he had been stabbed 193 times. However, when the police finally arrived, some five days after the murder, things did not look all that bad. The blood-soaked mattress and the equally bloody carpet had been removed and the room had been scrubbed with bleach before being given a fresh coat of paint.

All of this work had been done by Jeff's wife, Susan, who had then turned herself in. She did not hesitate to tell the police that she had killed her husband.

FRIENDLY

A 21-year-old former waitress, Susan Wyche met Jeff in

1997 on the beach at Galveston, Texas. Jeff was a friendly, energetic man who was always up for a night out with the boys. He was also no stranger to drugs or strip clubs.

Yet when Susan became pregnant he seemed willing to settle down, so they set up house together just outside Houston. Then in 1998, one month after their marriage, the newlyweds welcomed a son, Bradley. It was not too long before Susan and Jeff had a daughter, Kaily.

While Susan stayed at home with the children, Jeff worked as a carpet and tile salesman. However, Susan would later claim that her stay-at-home mother role hid a dark truth. Jeff had an irrational fear that she was cheating on him. As a result, he would not allow her to leave the house without his knowledge. She had to report her location to him at all times.

Not only that – things had to be just right at home. The presence of two young children was in no way an excuse for untidiness or dirt.

On 13 January 2003, Jeff returned home from a boxing lesson. Susan would later testify that he appeared to be under the influence of drugs. At some point, 4-year-old Bradley came crying to his mother: Jeff had hit him, he said. According to Susan, she then did her duty as a mother by putting the children to bed, before confronting her husband. She laid it on the line by saying that she would leave – and take the children with her – unless he got help for his anger and his drug problems.

KNIFE ATTACK

Susan said the ultimatum threw her husband into a rage. Jeff pushed her to the floor, kicked her several times in the stomach and then raped her. After the assault was over, she just lay on the bed, defeated, with her eyes closed.

Then she heard Jeff say, 'Die bitch.' She opened her eyes to see him standing over her with a knife. Jeff weighed nearly twice as much as she did and he towered over her by some eight inches. Even so, Susan claimed that she was able to push him aside and wrestle the knife from him. Because she feared for her life at that point, she stabbed him repeatedly until Bradley came to the bedroom door.

FOG DESCENDS

According to Susan's testimony, she then took a break from the killing. She saw her little boy back to bed before returning to the bedroom, where she continued to stab her husband. After that, Susan said, a fog descended on her: nothing seemed entirely clear or certain. She dragged her husband's body through the house and into the garden. Then she dropped it into a shallow hole that Jeff had dug. He had intended to install a fountain. As the week progressed, she kept on dumping potting soil into the hole. She thought it would weigh him down if he revived. Susan said that she dared not sleep because she was fearful that Jeff might walk through the doorway at any moment. The only reason she had scrubbed and painted the bedroom, she said, was that she had been afraid that Jeff would have been angry about the mess she had made.

After Jeff had been dead for five days, and it appeared that he was not coming back, Susan told her mother about the stabbing. DeGuerin Dickson & Hennessy, a prominent Houston law firm was hired and Susan was admitted to a mental health facility. It was not until that evening, after Susan's lawyer had contacted the district attorney's office, that the authorities finally found Jeff's body. It was a disturbing sight. The dead man was only partially buried. One hand had been chewed off by the Wrights' dog, though both wrists were still attached to the rest of the corpse, with neckties tied around each. An ankle had been tied with the sash from a bathrobe. Jeff's buttocks, thighs and genitals were covered in red candle wax.

JEFF'S SKULL

What appeared to be the murder weapon, a knife, was found in two locations: the handle and most of the blade were in a nearby flowerpot, while the tip of the blade was still buried in Jeff's skull. As far as the autopsy was able to determine, the dead man had been stabbed 193 times, though none of the wounds would have been fatal in themselves.

Later that day, Susan turned herself in.

NO INJURIES

Susan's trial began on 23 February 2004. The state's

argument was that her motivation had been Jeff's $200,000 life insurance policy. While there was no argument that the marriage had been unhealthy, the prosecution pointed out that Susan had never displayed any of the injuries that would have accompanied vicious assaults of the sort she had described to the police.

In fact, witnesses were brought in to testify that Jeff was a gentle man, who would not have raised a hand against his wife or his children. The prosecution also had an issue with Susan's description of the physical fight that had resulted in Jeff's death. They suggested that she simply did not have the strength to overpower her husband. The neckties and the sash, they said, were clear evidence that the dead man had been bound at the time.

'WEEK OF FOG'

Next, the prosecution came to the 'week of fog' that Susan had supposedly experienced. The idea was ridiculed. They pointed out that she had instead displayed extraordinary clarity of mind throughout that week. On the day after the murder, she had pressed charges against Jeff. He had been hitting her and Bradley, she said. She had also asked the neighbours to call the police if they saw her husband around the house.

Both of these actions, the prosecution said, were evidence of a manipulative mind at work. Not only that, she had removed Jeff's name from the message on the family's answering machine.

And, on top of that, she had cleaned out the cheque account she had shared with her husband.

The visit to the police had been a blunder, because it had led to a visit from child welfare officials before she was able to clean the bedroom and finish disposing of Jeff's body. Susan realized that she would have to change her plan, so she came up with the story of the long-term abuse.

HISTORY OF ABUSE

Much of the case for the defence rested on Susan's testimony. Though the accused had not shared such stories before the murder, she detailed a history of the abuse she had suffered at her dead husband's hands.

Jeff had unjustly accused her of cheating, yet he had conducted affairs of his own in the family home. She told the court that she had contracted herpes from her husband. Then there was his cocaine habit, which made the situation all the worse. And yet, Susan had swallowed it all – that is until Jeff began physically abusing their children.

'I stabbed him in the head,' she said, 'and I stabbed him in the neck and I stabbed him in the chest and I stabbed him in the stomach, and I stabbed his leg for all the times he kicked me, and I stabbed his penis for all the times he made me have sex when I didn't want to.'

On 2 March 2004 the jury of five women and seven men returned a guilty verdict. Susan Wright was sentenced to 25 years' imprisonment.

AILEEN WUORNOS
damsel of death

Many would say that the real-life exploits of Aileen Wuornos were sensational enough. Yet her case was still surrounded by a great deal of hyperbole.

In some media reports she was described as 'the first female serial killer', but that only demonstrates an ignorance of the facts. History is full of women who have committed multiple murders. Take Elizabeth Báthory, for instance, the 17th-century Hungarian countess known as the 'Bloody Lady of Cachtice'. She was convicted on 80 counts of murder, but some put her total at over 600.

To others, Aileen Wuornos was a 'lesbian murderer'. That is another false label, because it ignores the fact that she had displayed a marked preference for men as sexual partners. And at one time she had been someone's wife.

TURMOIL

The turmoil that surrounded Aileen began before she was even born. Her mother, Diane, was 15 years old when she married Leo, Aileen's father.

A little more than a year into the marriage, in March 1955, Diane gave birth to a baby boy who was named Keith. Shortly afterwards, Leo was arrested and charged with a number of petty crimes. However, he managed to avoid going to jail by joining the army. Pregnant with Aileen, Diane saw Leo's departure as an open door through which she could flee the marriage.

After giving birth to Aileen on 29 February 1956 she returned to her parents' Troy, Michigan home with her two children in tow. Four years later, she walked out of the door, leaving the two children for her parents to bring up.

Aileen would never see her father. In 1966, Leo was convicted of raping a 7-year-old girl and he was later diagnosed as a paranoid schizophrenic. He spent time in a number of mental hospitals before ending up in a Kansas prison cell. It was there that he hanged himself in 1969. Diane's parents then legally adopted Aileen and

Keith and they were raised side by side with Diane's two younger siblings. The Wuornos couple did not look like grandparents. Indeed, Aileen maintained that for most of her childhood she thought they were her true parents. It was not always a happy environment. She and Keith suffered beatings from her grandfather.

ON THE STREET

At the age of ten, Aileen began having sexual relations with Keith. Their encounters were witnessed by the neighbourhood boys. Within a year, she was having sex with boys other than her brother in exchange for cigarettes and small sums of money.

She used the cash earned with her body to buy drugs and alcohol. In 1970, at the age of 14, Aileen became pregnant. She claimed that an older man, a neighbour, had raped her. When her grandparents found out, she was sent to a home for unwed mothers. On 23 March 1971, she gave birth to a baby boy. The child was taken away for adoption without her ever laying eyes on him.

Four months later, her grandmother died of liver

failure. Her passing marked the end of Aileen and Keith's welcome in the Wuornos household. The two teenagers were told that they must leave the house immediately, never to return. They had no choice but to go their separate ways. Keith found a place to stay with friends in the neighbourhood, while Aileen turned to prostitution.

ON THE MOVE

Three years passed before Aileen came into contact with the law. However, her crimes at this stage had nothing to do with cash for sex. She was charged with drunk driving, disorderly conduct and firing a gun from a moving vehicle. A further charge of failing to appear in court was added after she returned to Michigan.

Aileen spent so much time moving back and forth across the United States that she was never in any one place for long. Then in 1976, at about the time of her twentieth birthday, she settled at Daytona Beach in Florida. Aileen had not been there long when she learned that the two most influential men in her life, her hated grandfather and her beloved brother, had died. While the old man had killed himself through gas inhalation, Keith's death was not of his own choosing. On 17 July, he had succumbed to throat cancer. As the beneficiary of his life insurance, Aileen received $10,000. Two months later, the money was gone. One of her purchases was a car, which she subsequently wrecked.

The only way was to go back to hitchhiking. Then in September she was picked up by a wealthy retiree named Lewis Fell. Although he was 49 years her senior, the two were married before the end of the calendar year.

The event even made the society pages of the local newspaper. Fell proved to be a most generous man. He bought his bride a brand-new car and expensive jewellery. She now had every chance of leading a stable life.

However, the marriage was neither peaceful nor enduring. Aileen was not able to change her behaviour. She drank heavily and she would pick fights in the local bars. One bar room encounter led to her being jailed for assault.

Nine weeks after the wedding, Lewis filed for divorce. He claimed that his wife had struck him with his cane after he had refused to give her more money.

ON THE GAME

Now that the marriage was over, Aileen returned to prostitution. She worked the exit ramps of the Florida highways. Without Keith to provide comfort and support, her behaviour became increasingly erratic.

In 1978, Aileen took a .22 calibre pistol and shot herself in the stomach. She was rushed to a hospital, where she received the very best in medical attention, but next to no counselling.

Aileen could never have been described as a beauty, but by now her average looks were fading with time, drink and drugs. As a result, her income from prostitution started to decline. Increasingly she turned to crime as a means of support. In May 1981, wearing only a bikini, Aileen held up a small supermarket in Edgewater, Florida. She was soon apprehended when her run-down getaway car overheated and broke down by the side of the highway. After being charged with armed robbery she spent most of the next two years in prison. Though much of her time was devoted to reading the Bible, Aileen did not emerge from jail a changed woman. Over the next two years, she was charged with attempting to pass forged cheques, speeding, grand theft auto, resisting arrest, obstruction and attempting to rob a boyfriend at gunpoint.

She once wrote that she turned to women as partners at the age of 28. The decision, she said, brought 'a world of trouble'. In the summer of 1986, while drinking in a Daytona gay bar, she met a 24-year-old motel maid named Tyria Moore. The two became lovers that same evening and they soon moved in together. Aileen encouraged Ty to quit her job, saying that she would support them both with her earnings as a prostitute.

The two adopted a transient lifestyle, which was a reflection of Aileen's success in trading sex for money. They bunked down in friends' apartments, abandoned trailers, motel rooms and, on occasion, the outdoors.

LOADED PISTOL

Sex between the two women became a rare thing, yet they stayed together.

If money permitted, they would go to bars or rent motel rooms and just watch television. Though Ty seemed content to be supported by Aileen, she was concerned about her companion's safety. Aileen took to working the streets and exit ramps with a loaded, concealed pistol.

By the autumn of 1989, Aileen was finding it difficult to support herself and Ty. The lack of money was having an effect on their relationship. Ty returned to work by taking on occasional jobs as a motel chambermaid, which made Aileen worry that her companion would leave her. She would later write that under this pressure she spun out of control.

'Hypnotically entranced in our companionship, so deeply lost in its same-sex relationship, causing me then to do the unthinkable.'

Aileen was referring here to the events of 30 November 1989. It was on that evening that Aileen committed her first murder. The victim, Richard Mallory, was the 51-year-old owner of an electronics repair shop. Mallory was on his way to Daytona Beach for a weekend of partying when he met Aileen. She then came up with the idea that he could pay her for sex. Mallory apparently agreed, so they drove into the woods outside the city. They shared a bottle of vodka and chatted until dawn. Then, quite suddenly,

Aileen pulled out her handgun and shot him four times in the chest and the back. She grabbed whatever money she could find, covered Mallory's body over with some carpeting and drove off in his car.

When she got home, Aileen told Ty what she had done. Ty did not believe the story until the news of the murder was reported in the media. Even then, she stuck by Aileen.

'I thought at that time: that, okay, she has all the frustration out of her system – for whatever reason she hated society – that she'll be okay. But obviously she wasn't. Obviously it was just the turning point, and she figured she got away with it once – she would keep doing it.'

MORE MURDERS

Six months after the Mallory murder, in May 1990, Aileen was hitchhiking when she was picked up by a 43-year-old heavy equipment operator named David Spears. Aileen shot him six times and then stole his truck, which she later abandoned. Then on 6 June she flagged down her next victim, 40-year-old Charles Carskaddon. Aileen shot the man six times and then took his gun, money and jewellery. She drove off in his car. After putting some distance between herself and the body, she abandoned the vehicle. Now that she had no means of transport she began hitchhiking again.

She was soon offered a lift by 65-year-old Peter Siems, a former merchant seaman who had devoted his retirement to Christian outreach. The back of his car was loaded with Bibles, but this did not stop Aileen from murdering him.

Aileen then stole Siems' car, as she had done with her other victims. However, this time she chose to hold on to the vehicle. It was a foolish decision – one that would lead to her capture.

On 4 July, Ty was driving Siems' stolen car when she took a corner too fast and rolled the vehicle. She and Aileen panicked. They asked a witness not to call the police and then they fled the scene before the emergency vehicles could arrive. Although Aileen had wrenched the licence plates off the car and thrown them into the brush the authorities soon realized that they had found the car belonging to Siems. Added to that, the witness was able to provide extremely accurate descriptions of Aileen and Ty.

Over the next five months, Aileen killed three more men. It had become clear to the authorities that they were dealing with a serial killer. In November 1990 a number of newspapers across Florida ran a story about the killings. They included sketches of the two women who had been seen walking away from Siems' stolen car.

As a result, Aileen and Ty were identified by a number of people. Sensing that the authorities were closing in on them, Ty made herself scarce while Aileen was buying alcohol. The younger woman travelled north out of the state to stay with her sister in Pittston, Pennsylvania.

BREAKTHROUGH

As 1990 drew to a close, the authorities experienced a breakthrough when they came across pawn shop records of some of the items that had been stolen from Aileen's victims. On 6 January 1991, Aileen was arrested at the Last Resort biker bar in Florida. At the same time, Ty was tracked down to her sister's Pennsylvania home. She later helped the police out by getting Aileen to contact her at the motel at which she was staying. The telephone calls were then recorded. By 16 January, Aileen had become so fearful that Ty would be implicated in the murders that she confessed.

'The reason I'm confessing is there's not another girl,' she said. 'I did it. There is no other girl.'

Aileen admitted to killing seven men, though she claimed to have done so in self-defence. She maintained that all of them had either raped her or had intended to rape her.

A full year passed before she finally went on trial for the murder of Richard Mallory. Several people were called by the prosecution, including Ty. It was only then that Aileen realized she had been betrayed. When her former lover took the stand she avoided all eye contact. The only witness for the defence was Aileen herself. Her testimony was erratic and unconvincing.

On 27 January 1992, the jury took less than two hours to find Aileen guilty of Mallory's murder. She addressed the jury as it was being led out of the courtroom.

'I'm innocent. I was raped. I hope you get raped. Scumbags of America!'

On the following day Aileen came out with several similar outbursts during the penalty phase of the trial. She was sentenced to death. Over the next two years, she pleaded guilty to two counts of murder and she entered no contest pleas on three more. Although she had confessed to murdering Siems, along with the others, she was not charged, because no body was ever found.

Then in July 2001, after more than ten years in prison, of which nine had been spent on death row, Aileen petitioned the court to put an end to the mandated appeals of her death sentence.

She testified that the murders had not been acts of self-defence, as she had originally claimed.

On 9 October 2002, Wuornos became the tenth woman to be put to death in the United States since the reintroduction of the death penalty in 1976. Two months before, she had begun writing a candid confession:

Dear Lord Jesus,
I know I've done some wicked things in my life, and Lord God, I know I deserve every bit of the rot of Hell.

BIBLIOGRAPY

'Andrews "Driven to Suicide Attempt by Guilt Over
    Death"', *The Times*, 12 July 1997

Badertscher, Nancy, 'Jury Selection Under Way in Lynn
    Turner Trial', the *Atlanta Journal-Constitution*, 8 Jan. 2007

Berger, Joseph, 'Soviet Emigre is Guilty in Ax Murder of
    Husband', the *New York Times*, 31 Jan. 1997

–, 'Woman Sentenced to Life for Ax Killing of Husband',
    the *New York Times,* 1 May 1997

Bienvenu, Melissa, 'Murder by Antifreeze', *Atlanta
    Magazine*, Apr. 2003, 90–3, 118, 120, 122–4

Bragg, Rick, 'Arguments Begin in Susan Smith Trial', the
    New York Times, 19 July 1995

–, 'Focus on Susan Smith's Lies and a Smile', the *New
    York Times*, 25 July 1995

–, 'Life of a Mother Accused of Killing Offers No Clues',
    the *New York Times*, 6 Nov. 1994

–, 'Psychiatrist for Susan Smith Defense Tells of a
    Woman Desperate to Be Liked', the *New York Times*,
    22 July 1995

BIBLIOGRAPHY

Brooks, Libby, 'Was It Really Murder?', the *Guardian*, 30 Aug. 2003

Burbank, Jeff, *Las Vegas Babylon: True Tales of Glitter, Glamour and Greed*. Stuttgart: Franz Steiner Verlag, 2006

Chisum, W. Jerry & Turvey, Brent E., *Crime Reconstruction*, St. Louis, MO: Academic Press, 2006

Cleary, Caitlin, 'In Northern W.Va., Arson-Killing has Everyone's Attention', the *Pittsburgh Post-Gazette*, 30 Mar. 2006

Collins, Marion, *Black Widow*, New York: Macmillan, 2007

'Convicted Murderer's Mother Convicted of Perjury', the *Gadsden Times*, 31 Oct. 2003

Curtis, Gene, 'Only in Oklahoma: Black Widow Enjoyed the Limelight', the *Tulsa World*, 27 Oct. 2007

Cyriax, Oliver, *Crime: An Encyclopedia*, London: André Deutsch, 1993

'"Dead" Woman Couldn't Outrun Her Secret', the *Miami Herald*, 15 Jan. 1983

Dorell, Oren, 'Miller Mum as Case Heats Up', the *News & Observer*, 31 May 2004

—, 'No Death Penalty in Miller Case', the *News & Observer*, 17 Nov. 2004

'Father Tells Murder Trial His Daughter "Could Have Said Anything"', the *Daily Telegraph*, 17 July 2007

'FBI Agents Nab Fugitive on a Fluke', the *Miami Herald*, 14 Jan. 1983

'Fear of Mother Led to Son's Role in Houston Slaying, He Testifies', the *Austin American-Statesman*, 21 Apr. 1999

'Fiancée Gets Life for "Road Rage" Murder', the *Daily Telegraph*, 30 July 1997

'Fianceé Held in Road Murder', the *Sunday Times*, 8 Dec. 1997

Fields-Meyer, Thomas, 'Plot Twist', *People*, 16 Mar. 1998

Findlayson, George D., John J. Robinette: *Peerless Mentor: An Appreciation*, Toronto: Dundurn, 2003

'Folbigg's Husband Rejects $200,000 to Tell All', the *Sydney Morning Herald,* 30 Nov. 2003

Foreman, William, 'Housewife Guilty of Hong Kong "Milkshake Murder"', the *Independent*, 2 Sept. 2005

Francis, Eric, *A Wife's Revenge: The True Story of Susan Wright and a Marriage That Ended in Murder*, New York: Macmillan, 2005

'Fugitive in Poisonings May Change Personalities', the
    New York Times, 16 Oct. 1980

Gibson, Dirk Cameron, *Serial Murder and Media Circuses*,
    Westport, CT: Greenwood, 2006

'Girlfriend Charged in Slaying', the *Fort Worth Star-
    Telegram*, 17 Aug. 2002

'Girlfriend Given 40-year Term for Murder', the *Fort
    Worth Star-Telegram*, 11 Mar. 2005

Glendinning, Lee, 'Inside the Mind of a Killer Mother',
    The Age, 25 Oct. 2003

Gowen, Annie, 'Couple Charged With Killing Ex-Spouse
    and His Wife', the *Washington Post*, 22 Feb. 2002

Grace, Melissa, 'Accused's Drunken Display', the *New
    York Daily News*, 12 June 2002

—, and Leo Standora, 'Ex-Beau Testifies Vs. Widow', the
    New York Daily News, 13 June 2002

'Guest Dies at Murder Mystery', Associated Press, 20
    Feb. 1998

Gurr, Stephen, 'Plot Revealed in Grisly Morgan County
    Discovery', the *Athens Banner-Herald*, 17 Apr. 2003

Hagedorn, Emily, 'Hit Man: Wife Planned It All', the

Cincinnati Enquirer, 12 Feb. 2004

Haines, Max, *Canadian Crimes*, Toronto: Viking, 1998

Hannah, Jim, 'The Case of Adele Craven', the *Cincinnati Enquirer*, 5 Dec. 2002

—, 'Craven Retrial Starts Today', the *Cincinnati Enquirer*, 12 Jan. 2004

Hays, Kristen, 'Woman Guilty of Stabbing Husband 193 Times', the *Washington Post*, 3 Mar. 2004

Hills, Lauren, 'Accused Murderer in Mon County Headed Back to Jail', the *State Journal*, 20 July 2007

—, 'Michelle Michael Found Guilty', the *State Journal*, 20 July 2007

'Husband-Killer Dies of Exposure After Escape', the *Los Angeles Times*, 27 Feb. 1987

Jackson, Rochelle, *Inside Their Minds: Australian Criminals*, Sydney: Allen & Unwin, 2008

'Jury Hears Details of Slain Man's Life as Testimony Begins', the *Fort Worth Star-Telegram*, 2 Mar. 2005

Kirsta, Alix, *Deadlier Than the Male: Violence and Aggression in Women*, New York: HarperCollins, 1994

Kleinfield, N. R., 'Death of an Emigre; A Macabre

Ending to a 26-Year Marriage', the *New York Times,* 16 May 1997

Lalor, Peter. *Blood Stain*. Melbourne: Allen & Unwin, 2002.

Lee, Cynthia, *Murder and the Reasonable Man: Passion and Fear in the Criminal Courtroom*, New York: New York University Press, 2003

Lewis, Paul & Wight, Douglas, 'I Was Road Rage Killer', the *News of the World*, 18 Apr. 1999

'Man Receives 22 1/2 Years in Slaying of Scientist', the *New York Times,* 16 May 1997

'Man Testifies that Wife Coolly Planned to Kill Spouse', the *New York Times*, 14 Jan. 1997

Marlowe, John, *World's Most Evil Psychopaths*, London: Capella, 2007

McGraw, Seamus, 'Cowboy Boots, a Scarf, and a Fatal Attraction', the *Record* (Bergen County, NJ), 3 Sept. 1999

McMurray, Kevin F., *A Family Cursed: The Kissell Dynasty, a Gilded Fortune, and Two Brutal Murders*, New York: Macmillan, 2007

McQuiston, John T., 'Scientist's Wife Arraigned on Federal Charge', the *New York Times*, 20 Apr. 1996

McVicker, Steve, 'Heartburn Can Be Murder', the *Houston Press,* 27 May 1999

Morris, Mark, 'Missouri Man's Love Story Ends in Murder, Suicide', the *Kansas City Star,* 26 Sept. 2000

Morris, Steven, 'Ex-Aide to Duchess "Stabbed Lover to Death"', the *Guardian*, 24 Apr. 2001

—, 'Someone's Going to Get Hurt', the *Guardian*, 16 May 2001

'Mother of Woman Convicted in Double Slaying on Trial for Perjury', the *Columbus Ledger-Enquirer*, 28 Oct. 2003

'Motorist Killed in Road Rage Stabbing', the *Daily Telegraph*, 4 Dec. 1996

'Murder Trial Woman "Victim of Lynch Mob"', the *Daily Telegraph*, 12 July 1997

'Murder Victim's Fiancée Ill', *The Times*, 7 Dec. 1996

'Murder Suspect Pleads Guilty to Embezzlement, ID Theft', the *Charlotte Observer*, 1 May 2007

'Murder Trial of Former Police Officer Under Way', the *Athens Banner-Herald*, 15 Apr. 2003

Murphy, Shannon, 'Sharee Miller, in Prison in the Death of Her Husband, to Marry Again – Behind Bars', the *Flint Journal*, 24 Mar. 2008

Neumann, Lin, 'Lover "Bragged" of Affair', the *Standard*, 2 Sept. 2005

Nichols, Bruce, 'Mentally Disabled Man Found Slain Reportedly Was Lured', the *Dallas Morning News*, 29 Aug. 1998

'No Cause Determined in Deaths of Borders', the *New York Times*, 19 July 1989

'Nurse's Murder Trial Set to Begin', the *Times-West Virginian*, 5 July 2007

O'Connell, Peter, 'Rudin Expressed Fear of Violent Death', the *Las Vegas Review-Journal*, 13 Mar. 2001

—, 'Rudin Trial Can Get Confusing', the *Las Vegas Review-Journal*, 25 Mar. 2001

'Officials Take Custody of Fugitive Hilley', the *Miami Herald*, 20 Jan. 1983

Paine, Donald F., 'Evidence Issues in a Church Love Triangle', *Tennessee Bar Journal*, 41:10 (Oct. 2005): 22–3

Pearson, Patricia, *When She Was Bad: Violent Women*

and the Myth of Innocence, Toronto: Random House Canada, 1997

Pearson, Perry, 'Former Pelham Policeman and His Wife Charged with Homicides After Child Custody Dispute', the *Shelby County Reporter*, 28 Feb. 2002

Pendergast, Jane, 'Details Emerge in Craven Killing', the *Cincinnati Enquirer*, 2 Aug. 2000

Rashbaum, William K., 'Woman Accused of Killing Husband and Dumping Body', the *New York Times*, 7 May 2000

'"Road Rage" Check Fails to Find Clues', the *Daily Telegraph*, 10 Dec. 1996

'"Road Rage" Stabbing Victim Dies', *The Times*, 3 Dec. 1996

Robbins, Trina, *Tender Murderers: Women Who Kill*, Newburyport, MA: Conari, 2003

Robinson, Carol, 'Former Pelham Police Officer to Plead Guilty in Two Killings', the *Birmingham News*, 15 Apr. 2003

—, and Adam Goldman, 'Couple Sought in Two Killings', the *Birmingham News*, 19 Feb. 2002

—, and Jon Anderson, 'Officer Suspected in Killings Fired', the *Birmingham News*, 21 Feb. 2002

Rosen, Marjorie, Eskind, Emily & Hume, Martha, 'In the Dead of the Night', *People*, 42:10 (5 Sept. 1994)

Rule, Ann, *Heart Full of Lies: A True Story of Desire and Death*, New York: Free Press, 2003

—, *Smoke, Mirrors, and Murder; And Other True Cases*, New York: Pocket, 2008

Rupinski, Patrick, 'Did Love End with Homicide?', the *Birmingham Post-Herald*, 2 Feb. 2002

Scott, Gini Graham, *American Murder*, Westport, CT: Greenwood, 2007

Sengupta, Kim, 'Lady Jane's Lies Fail to Save Her from Jail for Murder', the *Independent*, 17 May 2001

Snow, Robert L., *Murder 101: Homicide and Its Investigation*, Westport, CT: Greenwood, 2005

Spangler, Todd, 'Corpse (a Real One) Found After Whodunit Play', *Associated Press*, 26 Feb. 1998

Stout, David, 'Susan Smith's Lawyer vs. the Electric Chair', the *New York Times*, 21 July 1995

Szego, Julie & Cauchi, Stephen, 'Killing Them Softly', the

Age, 30 Aug. 2003

Taubman, Bryna, *Hell Hath No Fury: A True Story of Wealth and Passion, Love and Envy, and a Woman Driven to the Ultimate Revenge*, New York: Macmillan, 1992

'Tipped Beer Spilled Wife's Poisoning Plot', the *Charlotte Observer*, 13 Nov. 2005

'Tracie Andrews "Bit Fiancé in Nightclub Row"', *The Times*, 3 July 1997

'Tracie Andrews Tells of Night Her Fiancé Died', *The Times*, 15 July 1997

'Trial Set to Begin for Woman Accused of Killing Husband', the *New York Times*, 5 Jan. 1997

Vronsky, Peter, *Female Serial Killers: How and Why Women Become Monsters*, New York: Berkley, 2007

Wansell, Geoffrey, *The Life of Frederick West*, London: Headline, 1996

'We Were So in Love, Andrews Told Police', *The Times*, 10 July 1997

Whaley, Monte, 'Charges Against Ken Nelson Dismissed', the *Denver Post*, 13 Mar. 2008

—, 'Shawna Nelson: I Was Framed', the *Denver Post*, 4

Mar. 2008

'Witness Says She Doubted Tale of Attack', *The Times*, 4 July 1997

'Woman Admits Role in Poisoning', the *Charlotte Observer*, 8 Nov. 2005

'Woman Convicted in Life-Insurance Killing', the *San Antonio Express-News*, 28 Aug. 1999

'Woman Convicted of Killing Boyfriend', the *Fort Worth Star-Telegram*, 10 Mar. 2005

'Woman in Road Rage Case "Hid Murder Knife in Boot"', *The Times*, 2 July 1997

'Woman Who Played Dead Guilty in Arsenic Murder', the *Miami Herald*, 10 June 1983

Wong, Albert, 'Calls to Lover as Kissel Covered Up', the *Standard*, 12 Aug. 2005

—, 'Guilty', the *Standard*, 2 Sept. 2005

—, 'Kissel Murder Case Nears End', the *Standard*, 27 Aug. 2005

—, 'Kissel "Pain" Disproportionate to Injury: Doctor', the *Standard*, 13 Aug. 2005

—, 'Maid Defends Slain Banker', the *Standard*, 22 June.

2005

—, 'Milkshake Turned Murder Case Witness into a Baby', the *Standard*, 15 June 2005

—, 'Scotch Twist in Kissel Case', the *Standard*, 14 June 2005

Wuornos, Aileen, with Berry-Dee, Christopher, *Monster: My True Story,* London: John Blake, 2004

Young, David, 'Shawna Nelson Sentenced to Life Behind Bars', the *Greeley Tribune*, 4 Mar. 2008

—, 'Shawna Nelson's Friend Delivers Tale of Vengeance', the *Greeley Tribune*, 27 Feb. 2008